ᴛʜᴇQuotable
INTELLECTUAL

THE Quotable
INTELLECTUAL

| 1,417 | BON MOTS, RIPOSTES, AND WITTICISMS |

for ASPIRING ACADEMICS, ARMCHAIR PHILOSOPHERS

...AND ANYONE ELSE WHO WANTS TO SOUND REALLY SMART

PETER ARCHER

Aadamsmedia
Avon, Massachusetts

Published by
Adams Media, a division of F+W Media, Inc.
57 Littlefield Street, Avon, MA 02322. U.S.A.
www.adamsmedia.com

ISBN 10: 1-4405-0589-6
ISBN 13: 978-1-4405-0589-8
eISBN 10: 1-4405-0731-7
eISBN 13: 978-1-4405-0731-1

Printed in the United States of America.

10 9 8 7 6 5 4 3 2 1

Library of Congress Cataloging-in-Publication Data
is available from the publisher.

This book is available at quantity discounts for bulk purchases.
For information, please call 1-800-289-0963.

"I might repeat to myself slowly and sooth-
ingly, a list of quotations beautiful from
minds profound—if I can remember any
of the damn things."

—DOROTHY PARKER

"I hate quotations. Tell me what you
know."

—RALPH WALDO EMERSON

"An intellectual is someone who has found
something more interesting than sex."

—EDGAR WALLACE

CONTENTS

Dedication

For Linda and Jocelyn

INTRODUCTION

One afternoon in the 1930s, Dorothy Parker and Claire Booth Luce ran into one another at the front door of the Algonquin Hotel in New York City. Luce stepped back and gestured magnanimously toward the entrance. "Age before beauty," she cracked. "Pearls before swine," replied Mrs. Parker serenely as she glided through the doorway.

It's that sort of comment—witty, barbed, offhand that makes one wish life had a pause and rewind button. How many times have we all encountered a situation in which we could have used the perfect comeback or witticism, if only we'd had time to think about it?

Consider, for instance, another famous encounter, this between the notoriously antagonistic pair Violet Asquith and Winston Churchill, both members of the British Parliament. At a dinner party, as guests looked on in fascination, the two went at it, hammer and tongs, over questions of government policy until Mrs. Asquith's temper gave way.

"Winston," she snapped, "if you were my husband, I'd poison your coffee."

The future prime minister of Great Britain took a long drag on his after-dinner cigar and glowered at her. "Madam," he growled, "if you were my wife, I'd drink it."

How many of us would have thought to say that?

Well, if we can't think of such timely epigrams on our own, the least we can do is borrow from those who can. Hence the purpose of the volume you hold in your hand. Herein are contained quotations from the wildly famous to the justly obscure. Here are thoughts, wisecracks, meditations, japes, wheezes, sneers, eulogies, and observations on a wide variety of subjects. If you find yourself—as you may well—in a conversation in which you wish to give the impression of wit and erudition, drop these sparkling gems into the talk at regular intervals and enjoy the acclaim that will come your way.

There are a few preparations you must undertake for this sort of thing. Memorize quotes appropriate to the occasion—there's nothing more awkward than someone who opens his wallet to pull out a list of epigrams he hoped to employ during the evening.

Also, make sure you get the wording and the attribution right. It's embarrassing to quote, say, Marcus Aurelius on the pleasures of friendship only to have one of your audience point out that actually it was Cicero who said that and he wasn't talking about friendship but about old age.

But apart from these things, you'll find the quotations in this book useful in most social situations—icebreakers at parties, and a way to impress someone you've been wanting to invite out for a quiet drink and possibly a stroll in the summer moonlight after the party is over.

Bonne Chance!

PART I

ART

"There are three forms of visual art: Painting is art to look at, sculpture is art you can walk around, and architecture is art you can walk through."

—DAN RICE

ART

Let's face it: No one really understands why humans create art. Still less do we understand why we create the art we do—is there really an explanation for Abstract Expressionism? Nonetheless, intellectuals have expended a good many words trying to understand the strange, uniquely human propensity to express ourselves in words, in music, in drawing and painting, and in sculpture and architecture.

If you want to impress your friends, the next time conversation at the dinner table lags drop in one of these gems:

"Art is the imposing of a pattern on experience, and our aesthetic enjoyment is recognition of the pattern."

—ALFRED NORTH WHITEHEAD

"Art is the desire of a man to express himself, to record the reactions of his personality to the world he lives in."

—AMY LOWELL (1874–1925)
an American poet from Brookline, Massachusetts, posthumously won the Pulitzer Prize in 1926.

"I believe that if it were left to artists to choose their own labels, most would choose none."

—BEN SHAHN

"Art is a collaboration between God and the artist, and the less the artist does the better."

—ANDRE GIDE

"Let each man exercise the art he knows."

—ARISTOPHANES

"I don't believe in total freedom for the artist. Left on his own, free to do anything he likes, the artist ends up doing nothing at all. If there's one thing that's dangerous for an artist, it's precisely this question of total freedom, waiting for inspiration and all the rest of it."

—FEDERICO FELLINI

"Art, like morality, consists of drawing the line somewhere."

—G. K. Chesterton
(1874–1936)
a prominent Christian author who today is most widely known for the *Father Brown* detective stories.

"What I dream of is an art of balance."

—Henri Matisse

"Every artist dips his brush in his own soul, and paints his own nature into his pictures."

—Henry Ward Beecher

"Through all the world there goes one long cry from the heart of the artist: Give me leave to do my utmost."

—Isak Dineson

"The painting has a life of its own. I try to let it come through."

—Jackson Pollock

"We must never forget that art is not a form of propaganda; it is a form of truth."

—John F. Kennedy

"Creativity is . . . seeing something that doesn't exist already. You need to find out how you can bring it into being and that way be a playmate with God."

—Michele Shea

"I say that good painters imitated nature; but that bad ones vomited it."

—Miguel de Cervantes
(1547–1616)
is among the greatest writers produced by Spain and celebrated for his masterwork, *Don Quixote*.

I s art an expression of the thoughts and urges of its time? Or is it above these things and merely a reflection of the artist's inner drives and psyche? You can join in the conversation with these thoughts.

"I paint my own reality. The only thing I know is that I paint because I need to, and I paint whatever passes through my head without any other consideration."

—FRIDA KAHLO

"Art is on the side of the oppressed. Think before you shudder at the simplistic dictum and its heretical definition of the freedom of art. For if art is freedom of the spirit, how can it exist within the oppressors?"

—EDITH WHARTON

"Works of art, in my opinion, are the only objects in the material universe to possess internal order, and that is why, though I don't believe that only art matters, I do believe in Art for Art's sake."

—E. M. FORSTER (1879–1970) authored such well-known novels as *A Passage to India* and *Howards End.*

E very artist wants to be pure. Every artist wants to change the world through his art. (Every artist also wants to be paid full market value for doing so.) Even if you can't help them in this lofty aim, you can at least quote them.

"Every child is an artist. The problem is how to remain an artist once he grows up."

—PABLO PICASSO

"Art forms of the past were really considered elitist. Bach did not compose for the masses, neither did Beethoven. It was always for patrons, aristocrats, and royalty. Now we have a sort of democratic version of that, which is to say that the audience is so splintered in its interests."

—DAVID CRONENBERG (1943–) a Canadian filmmaker, has made such movies as *The Fly* (1986), *A History of Violence* (2005), and *Eastern Promises* (2007).

"What we play is life."

—LOUIS ARMSTRONG

ARCHITECTURE

Every artist is convinced that his medium of expression is not only the best possible aesthetic but that it is the only one. This accounts for the fact that the average artist has an ego the size of a Texas dust storm—and about as overwhelming. Architects, because they work generally on a large scale, are probably at the top of the ego tree among the creative arts. Thus the best way to approach a gathering of people talking about architecture is to drop a few words from the giants of the profession.

"The mother art is architecture. Without an architecture of our own, we have no soul of our own civilization."

—FRANK LLOYD WRIGHT

"Architecture is the learned game, correct and magnificent, of forms assembled in the light."

—LE CORBUSIER

"Architecture starts when you carefully put two bricks together. There it begins."

—LUDWIG MIES VAN DER ROHE

"Architecture is the reaching out for the truth."

—LOUIS KAHN

"Our architecture reflects truly as a mirror."

—LOUIS SULLIVAN (1856–1924) was one of the foremost American architects of the nineteenth and twentieth centuries.

"A modern, harmonic and lively architecture is the visible sign of an authentic democracy."

—WALTER GROPIUS

"A house is a machine for living."

—R. BUCKMINSTER FULLER

"A great architect is not made by way of a brain nearly so much as he is made by way of a cultivated, enriched heart."

—FRANK LLOYD WRIGHT

Not everyone holds the architectural profession in such reverence. Modern architecture in particular has taken a severe tongue lashing from critics. If you want to deflate an architect's ego—or, at any rate, reduce it to a manageable size—try one of the following:

"Architecture is the art of how to waste space."

—PHILIP JOHNSON

"Architects believe that not only do they sit at the right hand of God, but that if God ever gets up, they take the chair."

—KAREN MOYER

"In my experience, if you have to keep the lavatory door shut by extending your left leg, it's modern architecture."

—NANCY BANKS SMITH

"You have to give this much to the Luftwaffe: when it knocked down our buildings it did not replace them with anything more offensive than rubble. We did that."

—CHARLES, PRINCE OF WALES

"The architecture profession has lost a lot of its integrity, especially in the USA. The general architect here has no scruples, no ambitions."

—HELMUT JAHN

"All architecture is great architecture after sunset."

—G. K. CHESTERTON

"Architect, n. One who drafts a plan of your house, and plans a draft of your money."

—AMBROSE BIERCE
(1842–1914?)
an editor, journalist, and writer, a savage satirist whose writings reflect trends in American literature after the Civil War.

"What has happened to architecture since the Second World War that the only passers-by who can contemplate it without pain are those equipped with a white stick and a dog?"

—BERNARD LEVIN

"A doctor can bury his mistakes, but an architect can only advise his clients to plant vines."

—FRANK LLOYD WRIGHT

"Believe me, that was a happy age, before the days of architects, before the days of builders."

—SENECA

Architects love to be praised, and to hear their profession elevated to the greatest heights. There's no better way to flatter them, and to make yourself appear smart and well-educated, than to toss out something like the following:

"Architecture is music in space, as it were a frozen music."
—FRIEDRICH WILHELM JOSEPH VON SCHELLING

"Architecture is the work of nations."
—JOHN RUSKIN

"Architecture aims at eternity."
—CHRISTOPHER WREN

"Architecture has recorded the great ideas of the human race. Not only every religious symbol, but every human thought has its page in that vast book."
—VICTOR HUGO

"The job of buildings is to improve human relations."
—RALPH ERSKINE

"The principle of Gothic architecture is infinity made imaginable."
—SAMUEL TAYLOR COLERIDGE

"Architecture is inhabited sculpture."
—CONSTANTIN BRANCUSI
(1876–1957)
an internationally known Romanian sculptor, helped usher in the Modernist movement with his works.

"Ah, to build, to build! That is the noblest of all the arts."
—HENRY WADSWORTH LONGFELLOW

"We shape our buildings; thereafter they shape us."
—WINSTON CHURCHILL

DGARRICK THEATRE:CHICAGO

The rules of archi-tecture, are in constant dispute. When listening to arguments about the true art of building and the impor-tance of Vision in Architecture, casually comment along the fol-lowing lines:

"Architecture begins where engi-neering ends."

—WALTER GROPIUS

"Architecture is not all about the design of the building and noth-ing else, it is also about the cul-tural setting and the ambience, the whole affair."

—MICHAEL GRAVES

"Form ever follows function."

—LOUIS SULLIVAN

"To create architecture is to put in order. Put what in order? Func-tion and objects."

—LE CORBUSIER (1887–1965) was a pioneer of modern architecture, in the movement known as Urbanism.

"Light, God's eldest daughter, is a principal beauty in a building."

—THOMAS FULLER

"I don't think of form as a kind of architecture. The architecture is the result of the forming. It is the kinesthetic and visual sense of position and wholeness that puts the thing into the realm of art."

—ROY LICHTENSTEIN

"The rules of navigation never navigated a ship. The rules of architecture never built a house."

—THOMAS REID

"Even though I build buildings and I pursue my architecture, I pursue it as an artist. I deliber-ately keep a tiny studio. I don't want to be an architectural firm. I want to remain an artist."

—MAYA LIN

"If a building becomes architec-ture, then it is art."

—ARNE JACOBSEN

"A structure becomes architec-tural, and not sculptural, when its elements no longer have their justification in nature."

—GUILLAUME APOLLINAIRE

"I strive for an architecture from which nothing can be taken away."

—HELMUT JAHN

"An architect should live as little in cities as a painter. Send him to our hills, and let him study there what nature understands by a buttress, and what by a dome."

—JOHN RUSKIN

Architecture teaches us about the past in a way that no other records can. Perhaps that's one of its real values, you can remind others of this by quoting them something like this:

"If I had to say which was telling the truth about society, a speech by a Minister of Housing or the actual buildings put up in his time, I should believe the buildings."

—KENNETH CLARK (1903–1983)
an art historian and author, is best known for his 1968 television series "Civilisation."

"All architects want to live beyond their deaths."

—PHILIP JOHNSON

"Architecture, of all the arts, is the one that acts most slowly but the most surely on the soul."

—ERNEST DIMNET

"Architecture should speak of its time and place, but yearn for timelessness."

—FRANK GEHRY

PAINTING

From the moment Ancient Man, deep in the caves of Lascaux, lifted his brush to paint pictures of bison and deer on the rocky walls, painting has been among the most magical of arts. Not surprisingly, artists have had a good deal to say about it. There are two ways to participate in a conversation about painting. You can draw on your experience of years studying art, walking the galleries of the Louvre or the Prado, examining the paintings of Monet, Velázquez, Goya, and Leonardo . . . . Or you can casually drop into the discussion something like the following:

"Painting is the grandchild of nature. It is related to God."

—REMBRANDT VAN RIJN

"Painting is silent poetry."

—SIMONIDES

"There are painters who transform the sun to a yellow spot, but there are others who with the help of their art and their intelligence transform a yellow spot into the sun."

—PABLO PICASSO

"Art is either plagiarism or revolution."

—PAUL GAUGUIN

"The position of the artist is humble. He is essentially a channel."

—PIET MONDRIAN

"All art is an imitation of nature."

—SENECA

"I don't paint things. I only paint the difference between things."

—HENRI MATISSE

"There is nothing more difficult for a truly creative painter than to paint a rose, because before he can do so he has first to forget all the roses that were ever painted."

—HENRI MATISSE (1869–1954) widely regarded as one of the most important artists of the twentieth century, noted for his revolutionary use of color.

P ainters don't like to talk about money or the fact that they sell their art. Such conversation is considered vulgar, since Art should be above mere Commerce. (Asking a painter how much she or he sold a picture for is a bit like asking your grandmother how much she spent on your Christmas present.) If the subject does comes up, try one of the following quotations to ease the flow:

"I'd asked around ten or fifteen people for suggestions. Finally one lady friend asked the right question. 'Well, what do you love the most?' That's how I started painting money."

—ANDY WARHOL

"An amateur is someone who supports himself with outside jobs which enable him to paint. A professional is someone whose wife works to enable him to paint."

—BEN SHAHN

"Art is making something out of nothing and selling it."

—FRANK ZAPPA

N othing is more repulsive to the artist than the critic. To endear yourself to an artist, always have a few nasty things to say about critics, reviewers, and criticism in general.

"Painting, n. The art of protecting flat surfaces from the weather and exposing them to the critic."

—AMBROSE BIERCE

"Every time I paint a portrait I lose a friend."

—JOHN SINGER SARGENT

"The artist is not a reporter, but a Great Teacher. It is not his business to depict the world as it is, but as it ought to be."

—H. L. MENCKEN (1880–1956)
an American journalist, editor, and writer, is best known for his book *The American Language*.

"A painting in a museum hears more ridiculous opinions than anything else in the world."

—EDMOND DE GONCOURT

A rtists love to be asked why and how they paint. They won't necessarily give you an answer, but they love to be asked. To get the conversation going, try one of the following.

"The world today doesn't make sense, so why should I paint pictures that do?"

—PABLO PICASSO

"Only when he no longer knows what he is doing does the painter do good things."

—EDGAR DEGAS

"A man paints with his brains and not with his hands."

—MICHAELANGELO

"I experience a period of frightening clarity in those moments when nature is so beautiful. I am no longer sure of myself, and the paintings appear as in a dream."

—VINCENT VAN GOGH

"Painting is just another way of keeping a diary."

—PABLO PICASSO (1881–1973)
is sometimes denoted as the greatest artist of the twentieth century.

"A good painter is to paint two main things, men and the working of man's mind."

—LEONARDO DA VINCI

"Painting is the nail to which I fasten my ideas."

—GEORGES BRAQUE

"Art is the imposing of a pattern on experience, and our aesthetic enjoyment is recognition of the pattern."

—ALFRED NORTH WHITEHEAD

"I've been doing a lot of abstract painting lately, extremely abstract. No brush, no paint, no canvas, I just think about it.

—STEVEN WRIGHT

"Artists who seek perfection in everything are those who cannot attain it in anything."

—EUGENE DELACROIX
(1798–1863)
was a French nineteenth-century painter

"Every good painter paints what he is."

—JACKSON POLLOCK

Then again . . .

"Good painting is the kind that looks like sculpture."

—MICHAELANGELO

"I sometimes wonder if the hand is not more sensitive to the beauties of sculpture than the eye. I should think the wonderful rhythmical flow of lines and curves could be more subtly felt than seen. Be this as it may, I know that I can feel the heartthrobs of the ancient Greeks in their marble gods and goddesses."

—HELEN KELLER

"A sculptor wields the chisel, and the stricken marble grows to beauty."

—WILLIAM CULLEN BRYANT

SCULPTURE

The first thing any self-respecting sculptor will explain to you is that sculpting is much harder and more demanding than painting. The second thing is that he is unappreciated by critics—especially the ones who have trashed his last six shows. The third is that he'd never dream of creating his Art for anything so vulgar as money. Be ready to join in the conversation by quoting something along the following lines.

"Sculpture is more divine, and more like Nature,

That fashions all her works in high relief,

And that is Sculpture.

This vast ball, the Earth,

Was moulded out of clay, and baked in fire;

Men, women, and all animals that breathe

Are statues, and not paintings."
—Henry Wadsworth
Longfellow

"Sculpture is the art of the intelligence."

—Pablo Picasso

"I say that the art of sculpture is eight times as great as any other art based on drawing, because a statue has eight views and they must all be equally good."

—BENVENUTO CELLINI

(1500–1571)

the quintessential Renaissance figure: a goldsmith, sculptor, painter, and politician.

"A fellow will hack half a year at a block of marble to make something in stone that hardly resembles a man. The value of statuary is owing to its difficulty. You would not value the finest head cut upon a carrot."

—SAMUEL JOHNSON

"As paradoxical as it may seem a great sculptor is as much a colourist as the best painter, or rather the best engraver. He plays so skillfully with all the resources of relief, he blends so well the boldness of light with the modesty of shadow, that his sculptures please one, as much as the most charming etchings."

—AUGUST RODIN

If a sculptor seems to be getting a bit above him or herself, you can always comment along the following lines. However, if the sculptor picks up a hammer after you've quoted your authority, be ready to duck.

"Sculpture, a very noble art, is one that does not in the execution require the same supreme ingenuity as the art of painting, since in two most important and difficult particulars, in foreshortening and in light and shade . . . the painter has to invent a process, [whereas] sculpture is helped by nature."

—LEONARDO DA VINCI

(1452–1519)

was a poet, painter, sculptor, muralist, musician, scientist, mathematician, and writer.

"I did my sculpture as a painter. I did not work as a sculptor."

—HENRI MATISSE

Once they've convinced you of the superiority of their art over all others, sculptors are eager to explain their philosophy and methods. It turns out that there are exactly as many of these as there are sculptors, whether working in bronze or marble, wood, or wind. If you want to get them going for an entire afternoon, start them off with a quotation such as these.

"A piece of sculpture can have a hole through it and not be weakened if the hole is of a studied size, shape, and direction."

—Henry Moore

"There is no substitute for feeling the stone, the metal, the plaster, or the wood in the hand; to feel its weight; to feel its texture; to struggle with it in the world rather than in the mind alone."

—WILLIAM M. DUPREE

"Bronze is the mirror of the form, wine of the mind."

—AESCHYLUS

"Sculpture occupies the same space as your body."

—ANISH KAPOOR

"A hole in the block of a piece of sculpture is in most cases nothing but the expression of impotence and weakness."

—FRITZ WOTRUBA (1907–1975) was a prominent Austrian sculptor who created many works in the form of megalithic abstractions.

"The essence of a sculpture must enter on tip-toe, as light as animal footprints on snow."

—JEAN ARP (1886–1966) was a leading figure in the Dada art movement.

"As picture teaches the colouring, so sculpture the anatomy of form."

—RALPH WALDO EMERSON

"A great sculpture can roll down a hill without breaking."

—MICHAELANGELO

"Sculpture is the art of the hole and the lump."

—AUGUST RODIN

O ne thing many sculptors do agree on (particularly those who carve in stone) is that the form of the finished sculpture lies hidden in the material. Display your erudition and extensive knowledge of the art (even if you don't have any) by quoting one of the following.

"Within every block of wood and stone, there dwells a spirit, waiting to be released. Direct carving is a way of freeing the spirit—my own and that of the stone or wood."

—HAP HAGOOD

"The stone unhewn and cold

Becomes a living mould,

The more the marble wastes

The more the statue grows."

—MICHAELANGELO

"I saw the angel in the marble and carved until I set him free."

—MICHAELANGELO

T o impress any art-
ist and elevate the
level of your conversa-
tion, quote from one of
the masters of the art.

"There are two devices which can help the sculptor to judge his work: one is not to see it for a while. The other . . . is to look at his work through spectacles which will change its color and magnify or diminish it, so as to disguise it somehow to his eye, and make it look as though it were the work of another."

—GIANLORENZO BERNINI

"Where did I learn to understand sculpture? In the woods by looking at the trees, along roads by observing the formation of clouds, in the studio by studying the model, everywhere except in the schools."

—AUGUST RODIN

CINEMA

When writing of his experiences as a successful Hollywood screenwriter, William Goldman observed, "Nobody knows anything." Although many others have made similar observations about the essentially anarchic process of movie making, nonetheless, some 400 movies are produced and released every year. This is something of a miracle, considering the vast amounts of ego, money, and influence that are common currency in Hollywood. Tinseltown is first and foremost about appearance—substance is very low down on the list of things that matter there. So toss out something like these sentiments, and you'll be welcomed into the world of America's showfolk.

"Drama is life with the dull bits cut out."

—ALFRED HITCHCOCK

"[M]ovie-making is the process of turning money into light. All they have at the end of the day is images flickering on a wall."

—JOHN BOORMAN

"A film is—or should be—more like music than like fiction. It should be a progression of moods and feelings. The theme, what's behind the emotion, the meaning, all that comes later."

—STANLEY KUBRICK

"Cinema should make you forget you are sitting in a theater."

—ROMAN POLANSKI

"Of all our inventions for mass communication, pictures still speak the most universally understood language."

—WALT DISNEY

"Film is one of the three universal languages; the other two: mathematics and music."

—FRANK CAPRA

"A film is never really good unless the camera is an eye in the head of a poet."

—ORSON WELLES

"A director makes only one movie in his life. Then he breaks it into pieces and makes it again."

—Jean Renoir

"To be an artist means to search, to find and look at these realities. To be an artist means never look away."

—Akira Kurosawa

(1910–1998)

one of the pre-eminent directors in film history, made Japanese movies into a powerful artistic force.

Some people in the film industry, usually actors, take movies much less seriously than others. In turn, filmmakers are sometimes contemptuous of actors, feeling, no doubt, that movies would be fine if actors didn't have to be involved. Actors and directors unite in their denigration of the struggling screenwriter, who feels that he is the key to the entire process and wishes his pay would reflect that. Depending on whom you're talking to about the movies, you can drop one of the following lines.

"Acting: An art which consists of keeping the audience from coughing."

—RALPH RICHARDSON

"The length of a film should be directly related to the endurance of the human bladder."

—ALFRED HITCHCOCK

"What I've learned is that life is too short and movies are too long."

—DENIS LEARY

"I don't take the movies seriously, and anyone who does is in for a headache."

—BETTE DAVIS

"I never enjoyed working in a film."

—MARLENE DIETRICH
(1901–1992)
became the embodiment of sexy and sultry in such movies as *Shanghai Express* and *The Scarlet Empress.*

"I've made so many movies playing a hooker that they don't pay me in the regular way anymore. They leave it on the dresser."

—SHIRLEY MACLAINE

"The close-up says everything."

—MARLON BRANDO

"If you are directing, you have the opportunity to put your signature on the bottom of the frame. You have the opportunity to say, 'This is what I believe. That is my credo. That is what I wish to state.'"

—RICHARD ATTENBOROUGH

"At the end of the game, it's the director who will attract the actors and it's the script that will attract the director. It all starts with the screenplay."

—DAVID BROWN

"For me, movies should be visual. If you want dialogue, you should read a book."

—VILMOS ZSIGMOND (1930–) an award-winning cinematographer, has worked on such movies as *McCabe and Mrs. Miller* (1971) and *Deliverance* (1972).

"Anybody can direct, but there are only eleven good writers."

—MEL BROOKS

"Being a screenwriter is not enough for a full creative life."

—WILLIAM GOLDMAN

"Having your book turned into a movie is like seeing your oxen turned into bouillon cubes."

—JOHN LeCARRE (1931–) is the pseudonym of David Cornwell, a British writer of spy thrillers such as *Tinker, Tailor, Soldier, Spy* and *The Russia House*.

"Never judge a book by its movie."

—J. W. EAGAN

"There are three kinds of people: men, women, and actors."

—D. A. DORAN

"Movies are not scripts, movies are films; they're not books, they're not the theatre."

—NICOLAS ROEG

"I don't think you should feel about a film. You should feel about a woman, not a movie. You can't kiss a movie."

—JEAN-LUC GODARD

"The only really good thing about acting in movies is there's no heavy lifting."

—CARY GRANT (1904–1986)
born Archibald Leach, became the embodiment of the sophisticated, suave leading man in such movies as *The Philadelphia Story*.

"You know, when I first went into the movies Lionel Barrymore played my grandfather. Later he played my father and finally he played my husband. If he had lived I'm sure I would have played his mother. That's the way it is in Hollywood. The men get younger and the women get older."

—LILLIAN GISH

"Never treat your audience as customers, always as partners."

—JIMMY STEWART

"There are only three ages for women in Hollywood—Babe, District Attorney, and Driving Miss Daisy."

—GOLDIE HAWN

"Being a movie star is a rare job. Nobody gives you any guarantees that you'll get to do it forever. It's a very lucky and privileged position to be in."

—DIANE KEATON

"The dance that happens between an actor and a director is a very delicate thing . . . it's why people tend to work together on many films over and over."

—SYDNEY POLLACK
(1934–2008)
was the director of *The Way We Were*, *Three Days of the Condor*, and *Out of Africa*.

"Studio executives are intelligent, brutally overworked men and women who share one thing in common with baseball managers: they wake up every morning of the world with the knowledge that sooner or later they're going to get fired."

—WILLIAM GOLDMAN

"You're only as good as your last picture."

—MARIE DRESSLER

S ome people believe that the function of movies is to teach the audience. Others are of the opinion that if the movie doesn't bore anyone to death it's worked pretty well. Wherever you stand on the issue, in any gathering in southern California there's sure to be at least one person in your vicinity with the opposite view. Twit their sensibilities with one of these quotations.

"It's movies that have really been running things in America ever since they were invented. They show you what to do, how to do it, when to do it, how to feel about it, and how to look how you feel about it."

—ANDY WARHOL

"We learn how to kiss or to drink, talk to our buddies—all the things that you can't really teach in social studies or history—we all learn them at the movies."

—JACK NICHOLSON

"Every time I go to a movie, it's magic, no matter what the movie's about."

—STEVEN SPIELBERG

"A good film is when the price of the dinner, the theatre admission and the babysitter were worth it."

—ALFRED HITCHCOCK

"If my film makes one more person miserable, I've done my job."

—WOODY ALLEN (1935–)
has been hailed as one of America's foremost film directors for movies such as *Annie Hall* and *Hannah and Her Sisters.*

Over the years, directors, actors, and executives have adapted movies to the changing tastes of the public and the developing technology of the industry. Not that they've always been pleased about it. The following quotes will help you sound like you fit in with the glitterati who rove up and down Hollywood Boulevard.

"Adding sound to movies would be like putting lipstick on the Venus de Milo."

—MARY PICKFORD

"A wide screen just makes a bad film twice as bad."

—SAMUEL GOLDWYN

"Cinema is the most beautiful fraud in the world."

—JEAN-LUC GODARD (1930–)
is representative of the French New Wave movement in cinema with movies such as *À bout de souffle*, *Le Vent d'est*, and *Prénom Carmen*.

"Everybody's a filmmaker today."

—JOHN MILIUS

"I think cinema, movies, and magic have always been closely associated. The very earliest people who made film were magicians."

—FRANCIS FORD COPPOLA

"A story should have a beginning, a middle, and an end . . . but not necessarily in that order."

—JEAN-LUC GODARD

Nothing condemns a movie more to intellectual ridicule than success. If a lot of people like it and are willing to pay money to go see it, the thinking goes, it can't be much good. Occasionally, a movie critics hailed upon its release will become popular, at which point the same critics will find numerous flaws in the film they overlooked the first time ("The love scenes are *so* forced and predictable!") and denounce it as pandering to popular taste. From the standpoint of movie critics (especially those from the *New York Times* and the *New Yorker*), the best films are made by unknown Malaysian directors, filmed in Spanish on location in Guatemala, and released in only three theaters in the United States, two of which happen to be located on the Lower East Side of Manhattan and seat fifteen people each. If you want to sound sophisticated and knowledgeable when you're around movie people, quote one of these sentiments.

"If my films don't show a profit, I know I'm doing something right."

—Woody Allen

"If you don't like my movies, don't watch them."

—DARIO ARGENTO

"Even if I set out to make a film about a filet of sole, it would be about me."

—FEDERICO FELLINI

"Shoot a few scenes out of focus. I want to win the foreign film award."

—BILLY WILDER (1906–2002) was an American director who specialized in screwball comedies such as *Ninotchka* and *Some Like It Hot*.

T he cinema continues to fascinate and entertain us. And since everyone's always talking about the last movie they saw, the great special effects shot in the last scene, the wonderful acting job the star almost did . . . feel free to throw in some comments along the following lines.

"In feature films, the director is God; in documentary films, God is the director."

—ALFRED HITCHCOCK

"Film spectators are quiet vampires."

—JIM MORRISON

"A film is a petrified fountain of thought."

—JEAN COCTEAU (1889–1963) was one of a number of French film directors in the mid-twentieth century who were deeply influenced by surrealism, as evidenced by such films as *Orphée* and *Les parents terribles*.

"Cinema is a matter of what's in the frame and what's out."

—MARTIN SCORSESE

"The secret to film is that it's an illusion."

—GEORGE LUCAS

"There's only one thing that can kill the movies, and that's education."

—WILL ROGERS

"When you're making a movie, you can't think anybody will ever see it. You've just got to make a movie for the values it has. The greatest films were made because someone really wanted to make them."

—CLINT EASTWOOD

"A movie doesn't have to do everything. A movie just has to do a couple of things. If it does those things well and gives you a cool night at the movies, an emotion, that's good enough."

—QUENTIN TARANTINO (1963–) has been noted throughout his directorial career for his use of nonlinear storylines and ultraviolent scripts.

We'll let one of America's great comic talents have the last word:

"You know what your problem is, it's that you haven't seen enough movies, all of life's riddles are answered in the movies."

—STEVE MARTIN

PART II

LITERATURE

"Books are humanity in print."

—BARBARA TUCHMAN

THE NOVEL

Since the first novels were written in the eighteenth century, intellectuals have been proclaiming the death of the novel. Part of the reason for this, of course, is that it's much more exciting to announce the death or destruction of something than to celebrate its continuation. ("This year, novelists kept on writing novels. Way to go, guys!") As a matter of fact, today more novels than ever are churned out. Snooty intellectuals are therefore reduced to complaining about both the quality and the quantity of these productions, pointing out that the novels they like to read are hardly read by anyone—proving their worth. If you're caught in a discussion, sometime, about whether the novel is really dead, trot out something like this.

"If I were a writer, how I would enjoy being told the novel is dead. How liberating to work in the margins, outside a central perception."

—DON DELILLO

"Novels so often provide an anodyne and not an antidote, glide one into torpid slumbers instead of rousing one with a burning brand."

—VIRGINIA WOOLF (1882–1941)
was an English novelist and diarist as well as a central part of the Bloomsbury Group.

"The novel is always pop art, and the novel is always dying. That's the only way it stays alive. It does really die."

—LESLIE FIEDLER

"I find in most novels no imagination at all. They seem to think the highest form of the novel is to write about marriage, because that's the most important thing there is for middle-class people."

—GORE VIDAL

"Every author really wants to have letters printed in the papers. Unable to make the grade, he drops down a rung of the ladder and writes novels."

—P. G. WODEHOUSE

"The last time I was in Spain I got through six Jeffrey Archer novels. I must remember to take enough toilet paper next time."

—BOB MONKHOUSE

"Novels as dull as dishwater, with the grease of random sentiments floating on top."
—ITALO CALVINO (1923–1985)
wrote such novels is *Invisible Cities* and *The Baron of the Trees*.

"A person, be it gentleman or lady, who has not pleasure in a good novel, must be intolerably stupid."
—JANE AUSTEN

"People think that because a novel's invented, it isn't true. Exactly the reverse is the case. Biography and memoirs can never be wholly true, since they cannot include every conceivable circumstance of what happened. The novel can do that."
—ANTHONY POWELL

"Nothing induces me to read a novel except when I have to make money by writing about it. I detest them."
—VIRGINIA WOOLF

W riters are quick to explain that although the novel may be dead, dying, or decomposing, their novel will revive the discredited genre and instantly elevate them to the post of Recognized Genius. The chief enemies of such genius are the Critics, who are universally derided in all creative spheres. To ingratiate yourself at any gathering in which authors are present, savage critics by quoting something like the following.

"Any reviewer who expresses rage and loathing for a novel is preposterous. He or she is like a person who has put on full armor and attacked a hot fudge sundae."
—KURT VONNEGUT (1922–2007)
wrote novels that include *Slaughterhouse-Five, Cat's Cradle,* and *Breakfast of Champions*.

"I cringe when critics say I'm a master of the popular novel. What's an unpopular novel?"
—IRWIN SHAW

"Whatever I do is done out of sheer joy; I drop my fruits like a ripe tree. What the general reader or the critic makes of them is not my concern."

—HENRY MILLER

"It's with bad sentiments that one makes good novels."

—ALDOUS HUXLEY

"A novel that does not uncover a hitherto unknown segment of existence is immoral. Knowledge is the novel's only morality."

—MILAN KUNDERA (1929–)
a Czech writer who is best known for his novel *The Unbearable Lightness of Being*.

"They say great themes make great novels . . . but what these young writers don't understand is that there is no greater theme than men and women."

—JOHN O'HARA

"When writing a novel a writer should create living people; people not characters. A character is a caricature."

—ERNEST HEMINGWAY

"A good novel tells us the truth about its hero; but a bad novel tells us the truth about its author."

—G. K. CHESTERTON

"It's not a good idea to put your wife into a novel; not your latest wife, anyway."

—NORMAN MAILER (1923–2007)
an American novelist and journalist who blended reportage with opinion and personal experience.

"Great, big, serious novels always get awards. If it's a battle between a great, big, serious novel and a funny novel, the funny novel is always doomed."

—NEIL GAIMAN

"There are no laws for the novel. There never have been, nor can there ever be."

—DORIS LESSING

"The only reason for the existence of a novel is that it does attempt to represent life."

—HENRY JAMES

"What I couldn't help noticing was that I learned more about the novel in a morning by trying to write a page of one than I'd learned in seven years or so of trying to write criticism."

—PHILIP PULLMAN (1946–)
is best known for the trilogy *His Dark Materials*.

"Novel writing is far and away the most exhausting work I know."

—C. S. FORESTER

Novel writers and critics alike struggle to explain exactly what should and shouldn't go into a novel—no easy task, since they usually disagree on whether writing novels is even a worthwhile pursuit. One thing they do agree on is that writing a novel is beyond the poor abilities of most people and they shouldn't be encouraged to try. "It takes a lot of energy and a lot of neurosis to write a novel," said novelist Laurence Durrell. "If you were really sensible, you'd do something else." When a novelist starts complaining about the agonies of writing within your earshot, you can endear yourself to her or him by one of these quotations.

"Any fool can write a novel, but it takes real genius to sell it."

—J. G. BALLARD

"The great American novel has not only already been written, it has already been rejected."

—W. SOMERSET MAUGHAM
(1874–1965)
was known for his sarcastic sense of humor,
and his novels such as *Of Human Bondage*
became widely popular before World War II.

"There's no reason you should write any novel quickly."

—JOHN IRVING

"A good novel is worth more than the best scientific study."

—SAUL BELLOW

"Writing a novel is like making love, but it's also like having a tooth pulled. Pleasure and pain. Sometimes it's like making love while having a tooth pulled."

—DEAN KOONTZ

"Writing a novel is a terrible experience, during which the hair often falls out and the teeth decay."

—FLANNERY O'CONNOR

"A novel must be exceptionally good to live as long as the average cat."

—LORD CHESTERFIELD
(1694–1773)
a wealthy and politically powerful member of the British aristocracy, was noted for his witty epigrams.

"I can't understand why a person will take a year to write a novel when he can easily buy one for a few dollars."

—FRED ALLEN

"The really great novels tends to be the exact negative of its author's life."

—ANDRÉ MAUROIS (1885–1967)
composed biographies of prominent British figures such as Disraeli, Shelley, and Byron.

"Only in a novel are all things given full play."

—D. H. LAWRENCE

"It is the test of a novel writer's art that he conceal his snake-in-the-grass; but the reader may be sure that it is always there."

—ANTHONY TROLLOPE

"The first sentence of every novel should be: Trust me, this will take time but there is order here, very faint, very human."

—MICHAEL ONDAATJE

In the end, writers agree, they are at least as interesting as their novels. Hence the popularity of that peculiar book, the literary biography. In essence it is a long book written about someone who spent a long time writing books. But it gives writers—and you—a chance to comment extensively on their writing.

"Writing a story or a novel is one way of discovering sequence in experience, of stumbling upon cause and effect in the happenings of a writer's own life."

—EUDORA WELTY (1909–2001)
wrote short stories and novels about the American South that group her with William Faulkner as one of the great writers of Southern Gothic.

"The suspense of a novel is not only in the reader, but in the novelist, who is intensely curious about what will happen to the hero."

—MARY MCCARTHY

"My first novel took twelve years to complete because life got in my way."

—Donald McKay

"A novel has to have shape, and life doesn't have any."

—Jean Rhys (1890–1979)
Dominican novelist, wrote *Wide Sargasso Sea*, a "prequel" to Charlotte Brontë's Jane Eyre.

"A novel, in the end, is a container, a shape which you are trying to pour your story into."

—Helen Dunmore

"I had a romance novel inside me, but I paid three sailors to beat it out of me with steel pipes."

—Patton Oswalt

"The fundamental purpose of a novel like Count Julian is to achieve the unity of object and means of representation, the fusion of treason as scheme and treason as language."

—Juan Goytisolo (1931–)
is a Spanish poet and novelist who lives in Marrakech. His novels include *The Young Assassins, Count Julian*, and *Juan the Landless*.

"The novel is the highest form of human expression so far attained. Why? Because it is so incapable of the absolute."

—D. H. Lawrence

"A book is sent out into the world, and there is no way of fully anticipating the responses it will elicit."

—Chaim Potok (1929–2002)
was born to immigrant parents in Brooklyn, New York. His best-known book is *The Chosen*, published in 1967.

A nd a final word on the subject:

"Every journalist has a novel in him, which is an excellent place for it."

—Russell Lynes

POETRY

"Never leave me alone with the poets," *New Yorker* editor Harold Ross begged his staff. His sentiment is understandable: poetry is among the most confusing of arts. At least with novels it's a reasonably sure bet that you can hazard a guess at what the author meant. But poetry seems to take us into a new and dreadful world in which meanings are turned upside down, words and their definitions part ways, and every phrase seems to allude back to something else, only half glimpsed.

Poets themselves are not only aware of this ambiguity; they revel in it. Now you can revel with them (even if you don't understand them) by quoting one of the following.

"Most people ignore most poetry because most poetry ignores most people."
—ADRIAN MITCHELL

"It's easier to quote poets than to read them."
—ALLISON BARROWS

"A poem is no place for an idea."
—EDGAR WATSON HOWE

"Poetry is the deification of reality."
—EDITH SITWELL (1887–1964) shocked her aristocratic parents by her determination to shun their privileged lifestyle and become a poet.

"All slang is a metaphor, and all metaphor is poetry."
—G. K. CHESTERTON

"Poetry often enters through the window of irrelevance."
—M. C. RICHARDS

"Poetry is what gets lost in translation."
—ROBERT FROST (1874–1963) was an American poet, most often associated with New England, where many of his poems are set.

"Poetry is the journal of the sea animal living on land, wanting to fly in the air. Poetry is a search for syllables to shoot at the barriers of the unknown and the unknowable. Poetry is a phantom script telling how rainbows are made and why they go away."

—CARL SANDBURG

"Even when poetry has a meaning, as it usually has, it may be inadvisable to draw it out . . . . Perfect understanding will sometimes almost extinguish pleasure."

—A. E. HOUSMAN

"Poetry is a mirror which makes beautiful that which is distorted."

—PERCY SHELLEY

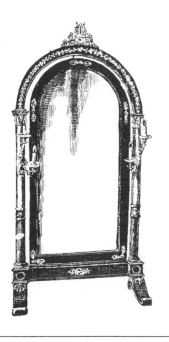

It's worth noting that Plato banished poets from his ideal Republic since they were purveyors of creative truth—not a welcome commodity in the kind of semi-totalitarian state he had in mind. Poets generally have been viewed in the same way Lady Caroline Lamb saw Lord Byron: "Mad, bad, and dangerous to know." The nicest thing you can say to a poet is, "You disturb me." If you want something a bit more eloquent to make them feel good, try one of the following.

"The worst tragedy for a poet is to be admired through being misunderstood."

—JEAN COCTEAU

"Poetry is nearer to vital truth than history."

—PLATO

"Poets are the unacknowledged. A poet is an unhappy being whose heart is torn by secret sufferings, but whose lips are so strangely formed that when the sighs and the cries escape them, they sound like beautiful music . . . ."

—SOREN KIERKEGAARD
(1813–1855)
wrote extensively in critique of the dominant Hegelian philosophy of his day and in support of Christianity.

"You don't have to suffer to be a poet; adolescence is enough suffering for anyone."

—JOHN CIARDI

"In science one tries to tell people, in such a way as to be understood by everyone, something that no one ever knew before. But in poetry, it's the exact opposite."

—PAUL DIRAC

"Poetry is man's rebellion against being what he is."

—JAMES BRANCH CABELL
(1879–1958)
an American fantasist and essayist, reached the height of his popularity in the 1920s.

"If Galileo had said in verse that the world moved, the Inquisition might have let him alone."

—THOMAS HARDY

"A poet's work is to name the unnameable, to point at frauds, to take sides, start arguments, shape the world, and stop it going to sleep."

—SALMAN RUSHDIE

"The poet doesn't invent. He listens."

—Jean Cocteau

"A poet is, before anything else, a person who is passionately in love with language."

—W. H. Auden

"All bad poetry springs from genuine feeling."

—Oscar Wilde

"A poet's autobiography is his poetry. Anything else is just a footnote."

—Yevgeny Yevtushenko (1933–)
was a Russian poet and novelist, often grouped with dissidents during the height of Soviet repression of artistic figures.

"A poet looks at the world the way a man looks at a woman."

—Wallace Stevens

"God is the perfect poet."

—Robert Browning

A nd how does a poet make poetry? Well, you can always ask. They're happy to tell you. And once you get some answers from them, such as the following, you can use them to impress others.

"Poetry is plucking at the heartstrings, and making music with them."

—Dennis Gabor

"Poetry is the art of uniting pleasure with truth."

—Samuel Johnson

"Poetry is the rhythmical creation of beauty in words."

—Edgar Allan Poe

"A poem is never finished, only abandoned."

—Paul Valéry (1871–1945)
was a French poet and essayist, was influential in the development of French belle letters prior to World War II.

"I was working on the proof of one of my poems all the morning and took out a comma. In the afternoon I put it back again."

—Oscar Wilde

"Poetry is not a turning loose of emotion, but an escape from emotion; it is not the expression of personality, but an escape from personality. But, of course, only those who have personality and emotions know what it means to want to escape from these things."

—T. S. ELIOT

"Poetry: the best words in the best order."

—SAMUEL TAYLOR COLERIDGE

I hope that clarifies things. But no matter how a poem comes to light, the most important point about poetry—at least according to the poets—is that it is superior to prose, and thus poets occupied a rarified sphere at the apex of the literary pantheon. You can pay them appropriate homage by dropping one of the following gems.

"One merit of poetry few persons will deny: it says more and in fewer words than prose."

—VOLTAIRE (1694–1778) born François-Marie Arouet, is the chief representative of the French Enlightenment of the eighteenth century.

"Poetry is all that is worth remembering in life."

—WILLIAM HAZLITT

"It is the job of poetry to clean up our word-clogged reality by creating silences around things."

—STEPHEN MALLARMÉ

"Poetry is just the evidence of life. If your life is burning well, poetry is just the ash."
—LEONARD COHEN

"There exist only three beings worthy of respect: the priest, the soldier, the poet. To know, to kill, to create."
—CHARLES BAUDELAIRE

"Poetry is a deal of joy and pain and wonder, with a dash of the dictionary."

—KAHLIL GIBRAN

In the event of a discussion of poetry becoming too exotic, always remember Oscar Wilde's wry observation.

"There's no money in poetry, but then there's no poetry in money, either."
—ROBERT GRAVES (1895–1985) is primarily known for his autobiography, *Goodbye to All That*, and for his novel *I, Claudius*.

"A poet can survive everything but a misprint."

—OSCAR WILDE

"Out of the quarrel with others we make rhetoric; out of the quarrel with ourselves we make poetry."
—WILLIAM BUTLER YEATS

DRAMA

"Drama," said the playwright Eugene Ionesco, "lies in the extreme exaggeration of the feelings, an exaggeration that dislocates flat everyday reality." Well, he'd know. Ionesco was one of the creators of the Theater of the Absurd, which has had a profound impact on modern drama. And it certainly exaggerates the hell out of reality (if you don't believe me, watch a production of *Rhinoceros* sometime). If conversation turns to the state of theater in the modern world, drop a few quotes to show how sophisticated you are.

"Theater is, of course, a reflection of life. Maybe we have to improve life before we can hope to improve theater."

—W. R. INGE

"The theater is so endlessly fascinating because it's so accidental. It's so much like life."

—ARTHUR MILLER (1915–2005)
was one of the preeminent American dramatists of the latter half of the twentieth century, with such masterpieces as *Death of a Salesman.*

"No theater could sanely flourish until there was an umbilical connection between what was happening on the stage and what was happening in the world."

—KENNETH TYNAN

"There are lots of young vital playwrights who are experimenting, and these are the plays that people who are interested in the theatre should see. They should go off Broadway. They should go to the cafe theatres and see the experiments that are being made."

—EDWARD ALBEE

"I think theater ought to be theatrical . . . you know, shuffling the pack in different ways so that it's—there's always some kind of ambush involved in the experience. You're being ambushed by an unexpected word, or by an elephant falling out of the cupboard, whatever it is."

—TOM STOPPARD

"The perfection in theater is that it's over the second it's done."

—WILLIAM HURT

"Thank God for the theater."

—RAUL JULIA

The theater is one of those things like God, art, or the Republican Party that intellectuals are always declaring dead. Despite this, every season, the theater gets out of its grave and walks down 42nd Street in New York. Still, if you want to appear hip and cool, quote something like these.

"I'm the end of the line; absurd and appalling as it may seem, serious New York theater has died in my lifetime."

—ARTHUR MILLER

"Theater people are always pining and agonizing because they're afraid that they'll be forgotten. And in America they're quite right. They will be."

—AGNES DE MILLE

"I think theater is powerful. The best experiences I had in the theater are more powerful than the best experiences I had in the movies."

—WILLIAM H. MACY

"The theater is the only branch of art much cared for by people of wealth; like canasta, it does away with the bother of talk after dinner."

—MARY MCCARTHY (1912–1989) critic and essayist, was deeply involved in the political left during and after World War II.

The biggest challenge to live theater is that it's, well, live. It's played in front of an audience who are impudent enough to have opinions about what they're watching. Just as it would be easier to publish books if they didn't have to be written by authors, so many actors and directors feel that if we could abolish audiences, drama would flourish. Show them you agree and are no mere spectator by quoting from the following.

"I write for an audience that likes what I like, reads what I read, thinks about the things I think about. In many ways, this puts me in opposition to the people who go to the theater generally."
—ERIC BOGOSIAN

"People wear shorts to the Broadway theater. There should be a law against that."
—STANLEY TUCCI

"You need three things in the theater—the play, the actors, and the audience—and each must give something."

—KENNETH HAIGH (1931–)

British actor, has been widely praised for his performance in John Osborne's play *Look Back in Anger* in 1956.

"It is a hopeless endeavour to attract people to a theatre unless they can be first brought to believe that they will never get in."

—CHARLES DICKENS

"If you really want to help the American theater, don't be an actress, dahling. Be an audience."

—TALLULAH BANKHEAD

"One of the things I love about theater, one of the reasons I'll never give it up, is that it's fifty percent the audience's responsibility."

—WILLIAM PETERSEN

"In theater, the wellspring of the character comes from the doing of it, like a trial by fire, but in front of an audience."

—ESTELLE PARSONS (1927–)

acted both on Broadway and in film and won an Oscar for a supporting role in *Bonnie and Clyde*.

"I made mistakes in drama. I thought drama was when the actors cried. But drama is when the audience cries."

—FRANK CAPRA

"As long as more people will pay admission to a theater to see a naked body than to see a naked brain, the drama will languish."

—GEORGE BERNARD SHAW

"The adrenaline of a live performance is unlike anything in film or theater. I can see why it's so addictive."

—GWYNETH PALTROW

S till, it can't be denied that Gwyneth Paltrow is right: there's something addictive about live theater. It brings together writing, acting, emotion, and immediacy. Sometimes it conveys a profound intellectual experience; other times it's just fun.

"When you come into the theater, you have to be willing to say, 'We're all here to undergo a communion, to find out what the hell is going on in this world.' If you're not willing to say that, what you get is entertainment instead of art, and poor entertainment at that."

—DAVID MAMET (1947–)
is a prominent American playwright whose plays include the award-winning *Glengarry Glen Ross* and *Speed-the-Plow*.

"A theatre, a literature, an artistic expression that does not speak for its own time has no relevance."

—DARIO FO

"From the start it has been the theater's business to entertain people . . . it needs no other passport than fun."

—BERTOLT BRECHT

"I want to give the audience a hint of a scene. No more than that. Give them too much and they won't contribute anything themselves. Give them just a suggestion and you get them working with you. That's what gives the theater meaning: when it becomes a social act."

—ORSON WELLES

"What people really want in the theater is fantasy involvement and not reality involvement."

—EDWARD ALBEE (1928–)
is best known for his plays
Who's Afraid of Virginia Woolf,
The Zoo Story, and *A Delicate Balance*.

"The drama may be called that part of theatrical art which lends itself most readily to intellectual discussion; what is left is theater."

—ROBERTSON DAVIES

"I think the cinema you like has more to do with silence, and the theater you like has more to do with language."

—BEN KINGSLEY

"God comes to us in theater in the way we communicate with each other, whether it be a symphony orchestra, or a wonderful ballet, or a beautiful painting, or a play. It's a way of expressing our humanity."

—JULIE HARRIS

"It's hard enough to write a good drama, it's much harder to write a good comedy, and it's hardest of all to write a drama with comedy. Which is what life is."

—JACK LEMMON

"Failure in the theater is more dramatic and uglier than any other form of writing. It costs so much, you feel so guilty."

—LILLIAN HELLMAN
(1905–1984)
wrote such plays as *The Children's Hour* and
The Little Foxes.

"A talent for drama is not a talent for writing but is an ability to articulate human relationships."

—GORE VIDAL

"The atmosphere of the theater is my oxygen."

—PLÁCIDO DOMINGO

LANGUAGE

Language is the meat and drink of intellectuals. They are—rightly—fascinated by its endless permutations and its amazing ability to convey thoughts over the span of thousands of years and tens of thousands of miles. Language holds the power of beauty, of anger, of inspiration, of hatred, and of knowledge. There's no better entry into the world of intellect than through the careful use of and appreciation for language.

"Language is the armory of the human mind, and at once contains the trophies of its past and the weapons of its future conquests."

—SAMUEL TAYLOR COLERIDGE

"Language is the archives of history."

—RALPH WALDO EMERSON

"Language is the soul of intellect, and reading is the essential process by which that intellect is cultivated beyond the commonplace experiences of everyday life."

—CHARLES SCRIBNER

(1854–1930)

joined his father's publishing firm after leaving college and continued to build it, making it one of the chief publishing houses in America.

"Language is not an abstract construction of the learned or of dictionary markers but is something arising out of the work, needs, ties, joys, affections, tastes, of long generations of humanity."

—NOAH WEBSTER

"Language is a cracked kettle on which we beat out tunes for bears to dance to, while all the time we long to move the stars to pity."

—GUSTAVE FLAUBERT

"Language is a skin: I rub my language against the other. It is as if I had words instead of fingers, or fingers at the tip of my words. My language trembles with desire."

—ROLAND BARTHES

"Language is the light of the mind."

—JOHN STUART MILL

"Language is the dress of thought."

—SAMUEL JOHNSON

(1709–1784)

was an English author and lexicographer, known for his compilation of the first major English-language dictionary.

"The tongue is but three inches long yet it can kill a man six feet high."

—JAPANESE PROVERB

"I personally think we developed language because of our deep need to complain."

—LILY TOMLIN

"Language is a virus from outer space."

—WILLIAM S. BURROUGHS

(1914–1997)

was a voice of the Beat Generation of writers and poets in the late 1950s and early 1960s, along with Ken Kesey and Jack Kerouac.

"Language is wine upon the lips."

—VIRGINIA WOOLF

Part of the fascination with language is that there are so many of them, and that they differ so widely from one another. The ideal intellectual speaks at least five languages and has a certain measure of contempt for anyone speaking fewer. If you don't speak that many—or any—you can at least let drop these pearls of wisdom.

"Those who know nothing of foreign languages know nothing of their own."

—JOHANN WOLFGANG VON GOETHE

"It is difficult for a woman to define her feelings in a language which is chiefly made by men to express theirs."

—THOMAS HARDY

"The only language men ever speak perfectly is the one they learn in babyhood when no one can teach them anything."

—MARIA MONTESSORI

"We are tied down to a language which makes up in obscurity what it lacks in style."

—TOM STOPPARD (1937–)
is the author of such plays as
Rosencrantz and Guildenstern Are Dead,
The Coast of Utopia, and *Arcadia*.

"Language is the tool of my trade, and I use them all—all the Englishes I grew up with."

—AMY TAN

"That woman speaks eight languages and can't say no in any of them."

—DOROTHY PARKER

"Americans who travel abroad for the first time are often shocked to discover that, despite all the progress that has been made in the last thirty years, many foreign people still speak in foreign languages."

—DAVE BARRY

"I am very sorry, but I cannot learn languages. I have tried hard, only to find that men of ordinary capacity can learn Sanskrit in less time than it takes me to buy a German dictionary."

—GEORGE BERNARD SHAW

"The quantity of consonants in the English language is constant. If omitted in one place, they turn up in another. When a Bostonian 'pahks' his 'cah,' the lost r's migrate southwest, causing a Texan to 'warsh' his car and invest in 'erl wells.'"

—ANONYMOUS

"In general, every country has the language it deserves."

—JORGE LUIS BORGES
(1899–1996)
one of the most influential writers of the latter half of the twentieth century, was an Argentinian essayist and poet.

LANGUAGE THROUGH NATURE
LITERATURE AND ART

PERDUE-GRISWOLD

It may not be possible for you to learn a variety of other languages, but pretty much everyone knows slang—which sometimes seems another language, especially to anyone over the age of fifty. Opinion on slang is divided. America has no institution such as the French Academy to man our linguistic ramparts, repelling new words. That's probably just as well, but with the onset of Textish (the peculiar shorthand associated with text messaging), one can't help feeling we've gone too far. Here are some thoughts that you can share on the subject of slang, profanity, and the misuse of language.

"It's a strange world of language in which skating on thin ice can get you into hot water."

—FRANKLIN P. JONES

"Slang is a language that rolls up its sleeves, spits on its hands, and goes to work."

—CARL SANDBURG

"Ours is a precarious language, as every writer knows, in which the merest shadow line often separates affirmation from negation, sense from nonsense, and one sex from the other."

—JAMES THURBER (1894–1961) was a major figure in American humor of the twentieth century, through his short stories and drawings.

"In certain trying circumstances, urgent circumstances, desperate circumstances, profanity furnishes a relief denied even to prayer."

—MARK TWAIN

"Swearing was invented as a compromise between running away and fighting."

—PETER FINLEY DUNNE

"By such innovations are languages enriched, when the words are adopted by the multitude and naturalized by custom."

—MIGUEL DE CERVANTES

"Man does not live by words alone, despite the fact that sometimes he has to eat them."

—ADLAI E. STEVENSON

"England and America are two countries separated by the same language."
—George Bernard Shaw

"But if thought corrupts language, language can also corrupt thought."
—George Orwell (1903–1950) was the pen name of Eric Blair, a novelist and critic, famous today for his novels *Animal Farm* and the dystopic *1984*.

"As societies grow decadent, the language grows decadent, too. Words are used to disguise, not to illuminate, action: you liberate a city by destroying it. Words are to confuse, so that at election time people will solemnly vote against their own interests."
—Gore Vidal

"The great enemy of clear language is insincerity. When there is a gap between one's real and one's declared aims, one turns, as it were, instinctively to long words and exhausted idioms, like a cuttlefish squirting out ink."
—George Orwell

"If names are not correct, language will not be in accordance with the truth of things."

—Confucius

L anguage remains
our most basic
means of communica-
tion, and one has to say
that, after evolving for
millions of years, it's
doing pretty well. At
least, no one's come up
with anything better.
And intellectuals have
excelled in pushing it
to the limits. You can
show your sophistica-
tion and your apprecia-
tion of their efforts by
effortlessly dropping
one of the following
into a pregnant pause
at dinner.

"I've always loved the flirtatious
tango of consonants and vowels,
the sturdy dependability of nouns
and capricious whimsy of verbs,
the strutting pageantry of the
adjective and the flitting evanes-
cence of the adverb, all kept safe
and orderly by those reliable little
policemen, punctuation marks.
Wow! Think I got my ass kicked
in high school?"

—DENNIS MILLER

"Dictionaries are like watches;
the worst is better than none, and
the best cannot be expected to go
quite true."

—SAMUEL JOHNSON

"A definition is the enclosing a
wilderness of idea within a wall
of words."

—SAMUEL BUTLER (1835–1902)
was a Victorian novelist, known for his works
The Way of All Flesh and *Erewhon* (a syllabic
reverse spelling of "nowhere").

"The finest language is mostly
made up of simple unimposing
words."

—GEORGE ELIOT

"Language is the most imperfect
and expensive means yet discovered for communicating thought."

—WILLIAM JAMES

PART III
MUSIC

"Without music,

life would be a mistake."

—FRIEDRICH NIETZSCHE

CLASSICAL MUSIC AND COMPOSERS

"If music be the food of love, play on!" says Duke Orsino in William Shakespeare's *Twelfth Night*. And what indeed would life be without music? For intellectuals, music should be approached cerebrally as well as emotionally and never confused with popular tunes. Dan Rather put it nicely: "An intellectual snob is someone who can listen to the *William Tell Overture* and not think of the Lone Ranger." The best musicians, therefore, are dead ones, who can't argue back against the interpretation of their works by critics. Classical music fits the bill very well for this sort of thing, with its pantheon of composers safely underground. If you want to quote musicians or about musicians—and you certainly should, since it shows you to be a person of taste and erudition—try one of these.

"If I should ever die, God forbid, let this be my epitaph:

The only proof he needed

For the existence of God

Was music."

—KURT VONNEGUT

"After silence, that which comes nearest to expressing the inexpressible is music."

—ALDOUS HUXLEY

"Music expresses that which cannot be put into words and that which cannot remain silent."

—VICTOR HUGO (1802–1885)
author of *Les Misérables*, became to many Frenchmen the embodiment of liberalism in the mid-nineteenth century.

"Music gives soul to the universe

Wings to the mind

Flight to the imagination

And life to everything"

—PLATO

"Music is the art of thinking with sounds."

—JULES COMBARIEU

"I think I should have no other mortal wants, if I could always have plenty of music. It seems to infuse strength into my limbs, and ideas into my brain. Life seems to go on without effort, when I am filled with music."

—GEORGE ELIOT

"Music is a discipline and a mistress of order and good manners. She makes the people milder and gentler, more moral and more reasonable."

—MARTIN LUTHER

"There's music in the sighing of a reed

There's music in the gushing of a rill

There's music in all things, if men had ears

Their earth is but an echo of the spheres."

—LORD BYRON (1788–1824) was a poet who commanded a rock-star following in nineteenth-century Europe with such poems as "Don Juan."

"Take a music bath once or twice a week for a few seasons, and you will find that it is to the soul what the water bath is to the body."

—OLIVER WENDELL HOLMES

It's true that some have taken a somewhat less elevated view of music and of musical instruments. The bagpipes in particular come in for some nasty hits for some reason. And some people's souls just aren't touched by beautiful harmonies.

"Music makes one feel so romantic. At least it always gets on one's nerves, which is the same thing nowadays."

—OSCAR WILDE

"There are some experiences in life which should not be demanded twice from any man, and one of them is listening to the Brahms Requiem."

—GEORGE BERNARD SHAW
(1856–1950)
a playwright, known for his biting satire as well as for his fierce convictions and for his vegetarianism, wrote *Pygmalion*.

"Anything that is too stupid to be spoken is sung."

—VOLTAIRE

"Musical people always want one to be perfectly dumb at the very moment when one is longing to be perfectly deaf."

—Oscar Wilde

"I don't know anything about music. In my line, you don't have to."

—Elvis Presley

"The Irish gave the bagpipes to the Scots as a joke. Unfortunately, the Scots haven't seen the joke yet."

—Oliver Herford

"Give the piper a penny to play and two pence to leave."

—English proverb

"I understand the inventor of the bagpipes was inspired when he saw a man carrying an indignant, asthmatic pig under his arm. Unfortunately, the manmade sound never equaled the purity of the sound achieved by the pig."

—Alfred Hitchcock

Before the magnificent array of great composers—Brahms, Beethoven, Bach, Handel, Mozart—intellectuals stand in awe. However, musicians themselves are notoriously insecure. Remember that it's all right to quote something nice about a composer to another musician—but only if the person you're quoting is dead.

"[Bach is] the immortal god of harmony."

—Ludwig van Beethoven
(1770–1827)
the pre-eminent composer of the early nineteenth century and was a major figure in the musical Romantic movement.

"Everything will pass, and the world will perish but the Ninth Symphony will remain."

—Mikhail Bakunin

"After playing Chopin, I feel as if I had been weeping over sins that I had never committed, and mourning over tragedies that were not my own."

—Oscar Wilde

"Handel is so great and so simple that no one but a professional musician is unable to understand him."

—SAMUEL BUTLER

"Handel was the Jupiter of music . . . his hallelujahs open the heavens. He utters the word 'Wonderful' as if all their trumpets spoke together. And then, when he comes to earth, to make love admidst nymphs and shepherds (for the beauties of all religions find room within his breast), his strains drip milk and honey, and his love is the youthfulness of the Golden Age."

—LEIGH HUNT

"O Mozart, immortal Mozart, how many, how infinitely many inspiring suggestions of a finer, better life have you left in our souls!"

—FRANZ SCHUBERT

(1797–1828)

Austrian composer, wrote a number of *lieder* (songs) and nine symphonies.

"Mozart should have composed *Faust*."

—JOHANN WOLFGANG VON GOETHE

"Bach almost persuades me to be a Christian."

—ROGER FRY

"You play Bach your way and I'll play him his way."

—WANDA LANDOWSKA

"[Beethoven] reminds me of a man driving the car with the handbrake on, but stubbornly refusing to stop, even though there is a strong smell of burning rubber."

—COLIN WILSON

"[Mozart] roused my admiration when I was young; he caused me to despair when I reached maturity; he is now the comfort of my old age."

—GIOACHINO ROSSINI

(1792–1868)

composed primarily operatic music, including, most famously, *The Barber of Seville*.

"Mozart is sunshine."

—ANTONIN DVORÁK

"I'm a revolutionary, money means nothing to me."

—FRÉDÉRIC CHOPIN

(1810–1849)

composed numerous symphonies and shorter pieces, mostly in the Romantic style then prevalent in Europe.

"I shall seize Fate by the throat; it shall certainly not bend and crush me completely.

—Ludwig van Beethoven

Mozart began composing when he was five years old and wrote his first symphony when he was seven. He can therefore serve as a useful reminder of the mediocrity of our own accomplishments. If you know someone who's getting above themselves, bring them down to Earth by saying:

"It is a sobering thought that when Mozart was my age he had been dead for three years."

—Tom Lehrer

OPERA

Opera might have been specially made for appreciation by intellectuals and the snobbishly elite. It's certainly beyond the comprehension of most ordinary people, since in its essence it consists of people singing about a story that no one in the audience cares about in a language that none of the onlookers understand. For this reason, people love to put on formal-wear and attend the opera, sipping champagne between acts and comparing this year's soprano in *Lucia del Lammermore* with the singer they saw two years ago at La Scala in Rome.

"At these concerts," George Bernard Shaw famously observed, "you will find rows of weary people who are there not because they really like classical music, but because they think they ought to like it." Despite the fact that no one understands the opera, (and that most don't like it) everyone still loves to talk about it. Join the conversation with the following quotes:

"Grand opera is the most powerful of stage appeals, and that almost entirely through the beauty of music."

—JOHN PHILIP SOUSA

"An opera begins long before the curtain goes up and ends long after it has come down. It starts in my imagination, it becomes my life, and it stays part of my life long after I've left the opera house."

—MARIA CALLAS (1923–1977)
was among the most acclaimed opera singers of the past century. She was also, as *Opera News* puts it, "the definition of the diva as artist."

"I have always believed that opera is a planet where the muses work together, join hands and celebrate all the arts."

—FRANCO ZEFFIRELLI

"Staid middle age loves the hurricane passions of opera."

—MASON COOLEY

"Any subject is good for opera if the composer feels it so intently he must sing it out."

—Gian Carlo Menotti

"Because, in opera, I have to sing for people that are very far from me, instead of when I sing a song, I try to imagine to sing like in an ear of a child."

—Andrea Bocelli (1958–) has tried to turn opera music into a popular art form, recording music with such stars as Sarah Brightman and Celine Dion.

"But nevertheless, it's music ultimately that matters in opera, and opera is a piece of music reaching out as a vision in sound reaching out to the world."

—John Eaton

"I would just like to say that opera is no longer about fat people in breastplates shattering wine glasses."

—Lesley Garrett

A ll that said, a surprisingly large number of people have found bitter things to say about the opera. It's curious, really, because not many people have actually attended an operatic performance, and even fewer seem inclined to give the experience a try. If you want to find something a bit more pointed to say about opera than "Turn off that damn screaming," try one of the following.

"Going to the opera, like getting drunk, is a sin that carries its own punishment with it."

—Hannah More

"I don't mind what language an opera is sung in so long as it is a language I don't understand."

—Edward Appleton

"No good opera plot can be sensible, for people do not sing when they are feeling sensible."

—W. H. Auden

"In opera, there is always too much singing."

—CLAUDE DEBUSSY
(1862–1918)
was a composer whose works are widely associated with the Impressionist school of music.

"I don't think an opera house is ever a place that can make you entirely happy."

—BERNARD HAITINK

"Of all the noises known to man, opera is the most expensive."

—MOLIÈRE

"Opera happens because a large number of things amazingly fail to go wrong."

—TERRY PRATCHETT

"Opera in English is, in the main, just about as sensible as baseball in Italian."

—H. L. MENCKEN

"Opera, next to Gothic architecture, is one of the strangest inventions of Western man. It could not have been foreseen by any logical process."

—KENNETH CLARK

"Opera? Just what the world needs: more fat women screaming."

—PETER BOYLE

"People are wrong when they say opera is not what it used to be. It is what it used to be. That is what's wrong with it."

—NOEL COWARD (1899–1973)
playwright, composer, and wit, was known for his light banter and charm, on display in his comic play *Private Lives*.

"The taxpayers cannot be relied upon to support performing arts such as opera. As a taxpayer, I am forced to admit that I would rather undergo a vasectomy via Weed Whacker than attend an opera."

—DAVE BARRY

"I wouldn't mind seeing opera die. Ever since I was a boy, I regarded opera as a ponderous anachronism, almost the equivalent of smoking."

—FRANK LLOYD WRIGHT

"Sleep is an excellent way of listening to an opera."

—JAMES STEPHENS

"The opera is like a husband with a foreign title, expensive to support, hard to understand, and therefore a supreme social challenge."

—CLEVELAND AMORY

"When an opera star sings her head off, she usually improves her appearance."

—VICTOR BORGE (1909–2000) was an accomplished pianist who turned his talents to comedy, making classical music both accessible and hilarious.

"Opera is where a guy gets stabbed in the back, and instead of dying, he sings."

—ROBERT BENCHLEY

Of all operatic words, those of Richard Wagner are probably the most widely known and the most extensively excoriated. This isn't too surprising, of course. Wagner was a notorious anti-Semite, much beloved by Adolph Hitler and the Nazis. His music is ponderous, and his masterpiece, *The Ring Cycle*, takes a week to perform. Indeed, for most Americans the name Wagner probably means Elmer Fudd singing "Kill the wabbit! Kill the wabbit! Kill the wabbit!" When the subject of Wagner's music comes up, you can hold your own with these comments.

"One can't judge Wagner's opera *Lohengrin* after a first hearing, and I certainly don't intend to hear it a second time."

—GIOACHINO ROSSINI

"I have witnessed and greatly enjoyed the first act of everything which Wagner created, but the effect on me has always been so powerful that one act was quite sufficient; whenever I have witnessed two acts I have gone away physically exhausted; and whenever I have ventured an entire opera the result has been the next thing to suicide."

—MARK TWAIN

"Is Wagner a human being at all? Is he not rather a disease? He contaminates everything he touches—he has made music sick."

—FRIEDRICH NIETZSCHE
(1844–1900)
a nineteenth-century philosopher, wrote about subjects such as the decline of religion and the rise of power.

"Wagner has lovely moments but awful quarters of an hour."

—GIOACHINO ROSSINI

"I have been told that Wagner's music is better than it sounds."

—MARK TWAIN

PART IV

SCIENCE

"If it's green or wriggles, it's biology.

If it stinks, it's chemistry.

If it doesn't work, it's physics."

—*Handy Guide to Science*

General Science

The sciences seem to have been in competition for quite some time to see which one is the scariest. Before 1945, chemistry was frightening because it was chemists who developed gas warfare in World War I and World War II. Then the atomic bomb was dropped on Hiroshima and Nagasaki, and the physicists became science's boogymen. Not only did they invent really powerful bombs, but as we learned from our local movie theaters, they created atomic radiation, which did things like revive corpses and turn them into zombies and mutate spiders into giant killing machines that destroyed Cleveland.

Nowadays, physics is still pretty nerve-wracking (so is Cleveland!). But before we turn to it, here are some general thoughts about science—its promises and limitations.

"Equipped with his five senses, man explores the universe around him and calls the adventure Science."

—Edwin Powell Hubble

"Science is the great antidote to the poison of enthusiasm and superstition."

—Adam Smith

"Science does not know its debt to imagination."

—Ralph Waldo Emerson

"There is something fascinating about science. One gets such wholesale returns of conjecture out of such a trifling investment of fact."

—Mark Twain

"The important thing in science is not so much to obtain new facts as to discover new ways of thinking about them."

—William Lawrence Bragg
(1890–1971)
was the director of the prestigious Cavendish Laboratory at Cambridge University.

"Science has made us gods even before we are worthy of being men."

—JEAN ROSTAND

"The saddest aspect of life right now is that science gathers knowledge faster than society gathers wisdom."

—ISAAC ASIMOV

"Science is simply common sense at its best."

—THOMAS HUXLEY (1825–1895)
a popularizer of Victorian science, was sometimes called "Darwin's bulldog" because of his fierce defense of the theory of evolution.

Science builds off theories and hypotheses, and, despite the cautions of others, scientists tend to become attached to theories. If you feel a scientist is becoming a bit dogmatic, you can always tell her something along the following lines.

"A fact is a simple statement that everyone believes. It is innocent, unless found guilty. A hypothesis is a novel suggestion that no one wants to believe. It is guilty, until found effective."

—EDWARD TELLER

"Great scientific discoveries have been made by men seeking to verify quite erroneous theories about the nature of things."

—ALDOUS HUXLEY

"The doubter is a true man of science; he doubts only himself and his interpretations, but he believes in science."

—CLAUDE BERNARD

"I have had my results for a long time, but I do not yet know how I am to arrive at them."

—KARL FRIEDRICH GAUSS
(1777–1855)

was a mathematician who contributed to numbers theory, statistics, and differential geometry, among other fields.

"Theory helps us bear our ignorance of facts."

—GEORGE SANTAYANA

"For every fact there is an infinity of hypotheses."

—ROBERT M. PIRSIG

"Science commits suicide when it adopts a creed."

—THOMAS HENRY HUXLEY

"In all science, error precedes the truth, and it is better it should go first than last."

—HUGH WALPOLE

PHYSICS

Physics is among the most intimidating of the sciences because it seems to deal with the very big—the way the universe works—on a macro scale. Fortunately, at least some scientists have tried to keep all this in perspective. It's hard to do this when they have to constantly remind the uninitiated that there are a billion stars in a galaxy and billions upon billions of galaxies in the know universe (not to mention the possibility of an infinity of universes—a statement that causes many listeners' eyes to briefly roll up into their heads before they stagger over to the bar and order another double Scotch). You can hold your own with physicists with something along the following lines:

"In science it often happens that scientists say, 'You know that's a really good argument; my position is mistaken,' and then they actually change their minds and you never hear that old view from them again. They really do it. It doesn't happen as often as it should, because scientists are human and change is sometimes painful. But it happens every day. I cannot recall the last time something like that happened in politics or religion."

—CARL SAGAN (1934–1996)
became known to millions of Americans through his award-winning miniseries *Cosmos*.

"Physics isn't a religion. If it were, we'd have a much easier time raising money."

—LEON LEDERMAN

"It should be possible to explain the laws of physics to a barmaid."

—ALBERT EINSTEIN
(1879–1955)
among the most important scientists who ever lived, revolutionized modern physics with his theories of special and general relativity.

"Physics is, hopefully, simple. Physicists are not."

—EDWARD TELLER

"In physics your solution should convince a reasonable person . . . . Ultimately in physics you're hoping to convince Nature. And I've found Nature to be pretty reasonable."

—FRANK WILCZEK

"All of my life I have been fascinated by the big questions that face us and have tried to find scientific answers to them. Perhaps that is why I have sold more books on physics than Madonna has on sex."

—STEPHEN HAWKING (1942–)
has been hailed as the most important physicist since Einstein.

All of this helps to place physics at the center of science. When talking to physicists, feel free to toss out something inspirational and uplifting, always remembering that physics started with the ancient Greeks.

"Give me a level long enough and a fulcrum on which to place it, and I shall move the world."

—ARCHIMEDES

"Not only is the universe stranger than we imagine, it is stranger than we can imagine."

—SIR ARTHUR EDDINGTON

"The effort to understand the universe is one of the very few things that lifts human life a little above the level of farce and gives it some of the grace of tragedy."

—STEVEN WEINBERG

"Magnetism, you recall from physics class, is a powerful force that causes certain items to be attracted to refrigerators."

—DAVE BARRY

"Physics is mathematical not because we know so much about the physical world, but because we know so little; it is only its mathematical properties that we can discover."

—BERTRAND RUSSELL

(1872–1970)

descended from an aristocratic and politically influential English family, became a mathematician and philosopher.

"In physics, you don't have to go around making trouble for yourself, nature does it for you."

—FRANK WILCZEK

"Physics is geometric proof on steroids."

—S. A. SACHS

"It would be a poor thing to be an atom in a universe without physicists, and physicists are made of atoms. A physicist is an atom's way of knowing about atoms."

—GEORGE WALD

"The whole history of physics proves that a new discovery is quite likely lurking at the next decimal place."

—F. K. RICHTMEYER

"The radical novelty of modern science lies precisely in the rejection of the belief, which is at the heart of all popular religion, that the forces which move the stars and atoms are contingent upon the preferences of the human heart."

—WALTER LIPPMANN

(1889–1974)

was an American journalist and commentator who had an immense political and social influence through his syndicated newspaper column.

"Physics is imagination in a straight jacket."

—JOHN MOFFAT

"The most exciting phrase to hear in science, the one that heralds the most discoveries, is not 'Eureka!' (I found it!) but 'That's funny . . . .'"

—ISAAC ASIMOV

BIOLOGY

For many years, biology was the unassuming wallflower sister of physics, patiently waiting in the wings, hoping that someone would ask her to dance. Charles Darwin ended that in 1858 when he published his book on the theory of natural selection in 1858. From that point on, biology has been a keen participant in scientific debate, provoking controversy that exploded in America in the Scopes trial of 1926 over whether Darwin's theory should be taught in high schools. More recently this argument has been reframed in the controversy over the teaching of "intelligent design."

Here are some thoughts to toss out if the discussion around your dinner table turns to the biological sciences.

"What can be more curious than that the hand of a man, formed for grasping, that of a mole for digging, the leg of a horse, the paddle of a porpoise, and the wing of a bat should all be constructed on the same pattern and should include similar bones, and in the same relative positions?"

—CHARLES DARWIN
(1809–1882)
was the originator (along with Alfred Russell Wallace) of the theory of evolution by natural selection.

"Biology is the science. Evolution is the concept that makes biology unique."

—JARED DIAMOND

"The essence of life is statistical improbability on a colossal scale."

—RICHARD DAWKINS

"Imagination reaches out repeatedly trying to achieve some higher level of understanding, until suddenly I find myself momentarily alone before one new corner of nature's pattern of beauty and true majesty revealed."

—RICHARD P. FEYNMAN

"To produce a really good biological theory one must try to see through the clutter produced by evolution to the basic mechanisms lying beneath them . . . ."

—FRANCIS CRICK (1916–2004)
together with James D. Watson, discovered the structure of the DNA molecule in 1953.

"Culture is how biology responds and makes its living conditions better."

—C. J. CHERRYH

"The fact of evolution is the backbone of biology, and biology is thus in the peculiar position of being a science founded on an improved theory."

—CHARLES DARWIN

"The capacity to blunder slightly is the real marvel of DNA. Without this special attribute, we would still be anaerobic bacteria and there would be no music."

—LEWIS THOMAS

"Nothing in biology makes sense except in the light of evolution."

—THEODOSIUS DOBZHANSKY

"[Natural selection] has no vision, no foresight, no sight at all. If it can be said to play the role of a watchmaker in nature, it is the blind watchmaker."

—RICHARD DAWKINS

"Creationist critics often charge that evolution cannot be tested and therefore cannot be viewed as a properly scientific subject at all. This claim is rhetorical nonsense."

—STEPHEN JAY GOULD

"The fundamentalists deny that evolution has taken place; they deny that the earth and the universe as a whole are more than a few thousand years old, and so on. There is ample scientific evidence that the fundamentalists are wrong in these matters, and that their notions of cosmogony have about as much basis in fact as the Tooth Fairy has."

—ISAAC ASIMOV (1920–1992)
wrote or edited some 500 books, including annotations of Byron and the Bible and the science fiction classic *Foundation* trilogy.

"Science has proof without any certainty. Creationists have certainty without any proof."
—ASHLEY MONTAGU

"Today, the theory of evolution is an accepted fact for everyone but a fundamentalist minority, whose objections are based not on reasoning but on doctrinaire adherence to religious principles."
—JAMES D. WATSON

"The proof of evolution lies in those adaptations that arise from improbable foundations."
—STEPHEN JAY GOULD
(1941–2002)
was an evolutionary biologist, best known for his theory of "punctuated equilibrium," a refinement of Darwin's theory.

"Evolution is not a force but a process. Not a cause but a law."
—JOHN MORLEY

"All the ills from which America suffers can be traced to the teaching of evolution."
—WILLIAM JENNINGS BRYAN

"A curious aspect of the theory of evolution is that everybody thinks he understands it."
—JACQUES MONOD

"Biology has at least fifty more interesting years."
—JAMES D. WATSON

"Today the theory of evolution is about as much open to doubt as the theory that the earth goes round the sun."
—RICHARD DAWKINS

MATHEMATICS

Math is a subject in which a person does either very well or very badly. Of all the subjects we study in elementary school and high school, it's probably the only one to give us anxiety attacks—apart from gym class. Perhaps the most perceptive comment was made by the German philosopher and poet Johann von Goethe (who was, himself, adept in mathematics), "Mathematicians are like Frenchman: Whatever you say to them, they translate it into their own language and forthwith it means something entire different." Or, as an anonymous commentator once observed, "Math is like love. A simple idea, but it can get complicated." Even if you failed basic geometry in high school, you can still hold your own by quoting from these words of wisdom:

"If people do not believe that mathematics is simple, it is only because they do not realize how complicated life is."

—JOHN LOUIS VON NEUMANN

"Mathematics are well and good but nature keeps dragging us around by the nose."

—ALBERT EINSTEIN

"I never did very well in math—I could never seem to persuade the teacher that I hadn't meant my answers literally."

—CALVIN TRILLIN (1935–)
served on the staff of the *New Yorker,* as well as writing for *The Nation.* His subjects have included politics, travel, and food.

"Arithmetic is where numbers fly like pigeons in and out of your head."

—CARL SANDBURG

"So if a man's wit be wandering, let him study the mathematics; for in demonstrations, if his wit be called away never so little, he must begin again."

—FRANCIS BACON

"The essence of mathematics is not to make simple things complicated, but to make complicated things simple."

—S. GUDDER

"Let us grant that the pursuit of mathematics is a divine madness of the human spirit, a refuge from the goading urgency of contingent happenings."
—ALFRED NORTH WHITEHEAD

"Music is the pleasure the human mind experiences from counting without being aware that it is counting."
—GOTTFRIED LEIBNIZ
(1646–1716)
is credited with the invention of the differential calculus at the same time as Isaac Newton, as well as other mathematical innovations.

"Anyone who cannot cope with mathematics is not fully human. At best he is a tolerable subhuman who has learned to wear shoes, bathe, and not make messes in the house."
—ROBERT HEINLEIN

"We could use up two Eternities in learning all that is to be learned about our own world and the thousands of nations that have arisen and flourished and vanished from it. Mathematics alone would occupy me eight million years."
—MARK TWAIN

"With my full philosophical rucksack I can only climb slowly up the mountain of mathematics."

—LUDWIG WITTGENSTEIN

Mathematics is one of the few sciences that keeps asking if its results mean anything. In a scintillating flight across the cloudless skies of the higher calculus, mathematicians are apt to lose themselves in the sheer aesthetic joy of their constructs, only to come to Earth later and start wondering if their equations have anything to do with reality. Should you come upon a mathematician sitting alone in a corner, white-knuckled hands wrapped tightly around a glass of campari and lemon juice, you can comfort her by quoting from the following:

"Mathematics is the supreme judge; from its decisions there is no appeal."
—TOBIAS DANTZIG

"The laws of nature are but the mathematical thoughts of God."
—EUCLID

"I used to love mathematics for its own sake, and I still do, because it allows for no hypocrisy and no vagueness...."
—STENDHAL (1783–1842)
was the pen name of writer Marie-Henri Beyle, whose masterpiece is *The Red and the Black*.

"As far as the laws of mathematics refer to reality, they are not certain; and as far as they are certain, they do not refer to reality."
—ALBERT EINSTEIN

"I like mathematics because it is not human and has nothing particular to do with this planet or with the whole accidental universe—because like Spinoza's God, it won't love us in return."
—BERTRAND RUSSELL

"Pure mathematics is, in its way, the poetry of logical ideas."
—ALBERT EINSTEIN

"Mathematics is the only science where one never knows what one is talking about nor whether what is said is true."
—BERTRAND RUSSELL

"In mathematics, you don't understand things. You just get used to them."
—JOHANN VON NEUMANN

All in all, economics may be stuck with the title of the Dismal Science, but mathematics is a close runner-up. That is, unless you talk for a few minutes to mathematicians, who are perpetually fascinated by the transcendent beauty of differential calculus and the joys of prime integers. Even if you can't make head or tail of what they're talking about, you can always impress them—to say nothing of other non-mathematically gifted folk—with one of the following quotes:

"Mathematics is the queen of sciences, and arithmetic is the queen of mathematics."

—KARL FRIEDRICH GAUSS

"What would life be without arithmetic but a scene of horrors."

—SYDNEY SMITH

"God does not care about our mathematical difficulties; He integrates empirically."

—ALBERT EINSTEIN

"For the things of this world cannot be made known without a knowledge of mathematics."

—ROGER BACON (1214–1294)
English monk and philosopher, was one of the founders of Empiricism, which holds that the foundation of knowledge is experience.

"The union of the mathematician with the poet, fervor with measure, passion with correctness, this is surely the ideal."

—WILLIAM JAMES

"The mathematical sciences particularly exhibit order, symmetry, and limitation; and these are the greatest forms of the beautiful."

—ARISTOTLE

"Why do we believe that in all matters the odd numbers are more powerful?"

—Pliny the Elder

"Uneven numbers are the gods' delight."

—Virgil (70 BCE–19 BCE) a Roman poet, exemplar of the Golden Age of classical Latin, was author of *The Aeneid*.

"One of the endlessly alluring aspects of mathematics is that its thorniest paradoxes have a way of blooming into beautiful theories."

—Philip J. Davis

"Pure mathematics is the world's best game. It is more absorbing than chess, more of a gamble than poker, and lasts longer than Monopoly. It's free. It can be played anywhere—Archimedes did it in a bathtub."

—Richard J. Trudeau

"Twice two makes four seems to me simply a piece of insolence. Twice two makes four is a pert coxcomb who stands with arms akimbo barring your path and spitting. I admit that twice two makes four is an excellent thing, but if we are to give everything its due, twice two makes five is sometimes a very charming thing too."

—Fyodor Dostoevsky

"I don't believe in mathematics."

—Albert Einstein

PART V

POLITICS, HISTORY, AND GOVERNMENT

"Man is by nature a political animal."

—ARISTOTLE

POLITICS AND GOVERNMENT

One January afternoon in the tumultuous and gloomy year of 1933, someone stepped into the dining room at the Algonquin Hotel in New York City and announced to those gathered around its famous Round Table, "Well, Calvin Coolidge is dead."

There was silence for a few moments, and then Dorothy Parker lifted her lovely dark eyes and soft, innocent face.

"How can you tell?" she asked.

Americans have always had a touch and go relationship with their politicians. Political complaint is one of the chief forms of American entertainment, and there's no sign of it losing its popularity. ("A statesman is a dead politician," opined cartoonist Berkley Breathed. "Lord knows, we need more statesmen!") After all, as we look at the array of political lunatics infesting Washington and the various state capitals, we can remind ourselves that it's always nice to have someone to feel superior to.

When dinner table talk turns to politics, throw out something like the following:

"A politician needs the ability to foretell what is going to happen tomorrow, next week, next month, and next year. And to have the ability afterwards to explain why it didn't happen."
—WINSTON CHURCHILL

"Too bad that all the people who really know how to run the country are busy driving taxi cabs and cutting hair."
—GEORGE BURNS

"I have come to the conclusion that politics are too serious a matter to be left to the politicians."

—CHARLES DE GAULLE

"Nothing is so admirable in politics as a short memory."

—JOHN KENNETH GALBRAITH
(1908–2006)
was leading figure in American Keynesian economics and an advisor to President John F. Kennedy.

"Politics is the art of the possible."

—OTTO VON BISMARCK

"Politics is supposed to be the second-oldest profession. I have come to realize that it bears a very close resemblance to the first."

—RONALD REAGAN

"A politician is a fellow who will lay down your life for his country."

—TEXAS GUINAN

"A politician is a statesman who approaches every question with an open mouth."

—ADLAI STEVENSON

"Politics is the art of looking for trouble, finding it everywhere, diagnosing it incorrectly, and applying the wrong remedies.

—GROUCHO MARX (1890–1977) together with his brothers Harpo and Chico, created sparkling gems of American humor in films such as *Duck Soup* and *Night at the Opera*.

"Truthfulness has never been counted among the political virtues, and lies have always been regarded as justifiable tools in political dealings."

—HANNAH ARENDT

"Politics, n. A strife of interests masquerading as a contest of principles. The conduct of public affairs for private advantage."

—AMBROSE BIERCE

"Ninety-eight percent of the adults in this country are decent, hardworking, honest Americans. It's the other lousy two percent that get all the publicity. But then, we elected them."

—LILY TOMLIN (1939–) is a comedic actress with a long career behind her, both in the movies and on stage.

"When I entered politics, I took the only downward turn you could take from journalism."

—JIM HIGHTOWER

A big part of the problem with politics is that we keep electing politicians. And since the day that the first Neanderthal politician lumbered forth from his cave to offer his fellow cavemen extra pelts if they'd vote him in as Chief Mastodon Basher, politicians have been on the take. Should anyone lose sight of that—though it's hard to forget—remind them by quoting something like these:

"Wherefore being all of one mind, we do highly resolve that government of the grafted by the grafter for the grafter shall not perish from the earth."

—MARK TWAIN

"Politicians are the same all over. They promise to build a bridge even where there is no river."

—NIKITA KRUSHCHEV

"A politician is a man who will double cross that bridge when he comes to it."

—OSCAR LEVANT

"We hang the petty thieves and appoint the great ones to public office."

—AESOP (CA. 620 BCE–564 BCE)
compiled a collection of fables, few of which he probably wrote.

"There is one safeguard known generally to the wise, which is an advantage and security to all, but especially to democracies as against despots. What is it? Distrust."

—DEMOSTHENES

"The work of the political activist inevitably involves a certain tension between the requirement that position be taken on current issues as they arise and the desire that one's contributions will somehow survive the ravages of time."

—ANGELA DAVIS

"Democracy means simply the bludgeoning of the people by the people for the people."

—OSCAR WILDE (1854–1900)
was known for his flamboyant lifestyle as well as for his clever epigrams, satirizing the Victorian age.

I'm not saying that there isn't still some idealism left in the political arena. If you're afraid of being too cynical (although when it comes to politics, cynicism is the default mode of most intellectuals), try one of these quotes to soften the mood.

"Public sentiment is everything. With public sentiment nothing can fail; without it nothing can succeed. He who molds public sentiment goes deeper than he who enacts statutes or decisions possible or impossible to execute."
—ABRAHAM LINCOLN

"The true test of the American ideal is whether we're able to recognize our failings and then rise together to meet the challenges of our time. Whether we allow ourselves to be shaped by events and history, or whether we act to shape them."
—BARACK OBAMA

"Ideas are great arrows, but there has to be a bow. And politics is the bow of idealism."
—BILL MOYERS

"To put the world right in order, we must first put the nation in order; to put the nation in order, we must first put the family in order; to put the family in order, we must first cultivate our personal life; we must first set our hearts right."
—CONFUCIUS

"In politics, an organized minority is a political majority."
—JESSE JACKSON (1941–)
is an African-American activist.

"The sad duty of politics is to establish justice in a sinful world."
—JIMMY CARTER

"There are times in politics when you must be on the right side and lose."

—JOHN KENNETH GALBRAITH

"Political convulsions, like geological upheavings, usher in new epochs of the world's progress."

—WENDELL PHILLIPS

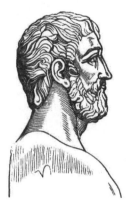

"The price of apathy towards public affairs is to be ruled by evil men."

—PLATO (428 BCE–348 BCE) perhaps, the most influential philosopher who ever lived, founded the Academy.

It's during election season when politics is at its most depressing—or entertaining, depending on your viewpoint. If you want to show your interest in and detachment from the prevailing political winds, quote something along these lines:

"If God wanted us to vote, he would have given us candidates."

—JAY LENO

"Whenever a man has cast a longing eye on offices, a rottenness begins in his conduct."

—THOMAS JEFFERSON

"A politician should have three hats. One for throwing into the ring, one for talking through, and one for pulling rabbits out of if elected."

—CARL SANDBURG (1878–1967) was a poet who attempted to distill the American spirit and experience in such poems as "Chicago."

"In war you can only be killed once, but in politics many times."

—WINSTON CHURCHILL

"Anyone that wants the presidency so much that he'll spend two years organizing and campaigning for it is not to be trusted with the office."

—DAVID BRODER

"An election is coming. Universal peace is declared, and the foxes have a sincere interest in prolonging the lives of the poultry."

—GEORGE ELIOT (1819–1880)
is the pseudonym of Mary Anne Evans, a novelist who wrote books such as *Middlemarch*.

"A national political campaign is better than the best circus ever heard of, with a mass baptism and a couple of hangings thrown in."

—H. L. MENCKEN

"Good thing we've still got politics in Texas—finest form of free entertainment ever invented."

—MOLLY IVINS

"In our brief national history we have shot four of our presidents, worried five of them to death, impeached one, and hounded another out of office. And when all else fails, we hold an election and assassinate their character."

—P. J. O'ROURKE

S ooner or later any political discussion, particularly one fueled by cocktails, is going to divide into a minimum of two camps: Democrats and Republicans. You can stand above the fray by throwing out observations about both parties.

"The Democrats are the party that says government will make you smarter, taller, richer, and remove the crabgrass on your lawn. The Republicans are the party that says government doesn't work and then they get elected and prove it."

—P. J. O'ROURKE (1947–)
is a humorist and journalist, distinguished by his libertarianism and economic conservatism.

"I recognize the Republican Party as the sheet anchor of the colored man's political hopes and the ark of his safety."

—FREDERICK DOUGLASS

"A conserva-
tive is one
who admires
radicals cen-
turies after
they're dead."

—LEO ROSTEN

"The Democrats seem to be basi-
cally nicer people, but they have
demonstrated time and again that
they have the management skills
of celery. They're the kind of people who'd stop to help you change
a flat, but would somehow man-
age to set your car on fire. I would
be reluctant to entrust them with
a Cuisinart, let alone the econ-
omy. The Republicans, on the
other hand, would know how to
fix your tire, but they wouldn't
bother to stop because they'd
want to be on time for Ugly Pants
Night at the country club."

—DAVE BARRY

"Thinking about profound social
change, conservatives always
expect disaster, while revolution-
aries confidentially expect utopia.
Both are wrong."

—CAROLYN HEILBRUN
(1926–2003)

was a scholar and professor at New York University, as well as author of a series of mystery
novels under the pseudonym Amanda Cross.

Politics is an inevitable part of American life. It's also free entertainment, not to mention a determining factor in shaping the life of the nation for the future. Though it's most fun to indulge in politics around election time, it's a subject that's also been known at any time of the year to bring congenial dinner parties to crashing conclusions, as the room separates into liberals and conservatives (with libertarians exiled to the balcony by both sides). If you want to lighten the mood under such circumstances, try tossing out a quote or two.

"In our age there is no such thing as 'keeping out of politics.' All issues are political issues, and politics itself is a mass of lies, evasions, folly, hatred, and schizophrenia."
—GEORGE ORWELL

"You can't ignore politics, no matter how much you'd like to."

—MOLLY IVINS

WAR

"War," the German military theoretician Karl von Clauswitz observed, "is politics by other means." And while almost all politicians can be counted upon to denounce war, none seem to have found a method of preventing it. In fact, some have spent a lot of time figuring out how to present it in the most favorable light. The most naked statement of this was made by Adolph Hitler's comrade Hermann Goering:

"Naturally the common people don't want war; neither in Russia, nor in England, nor in America, nor in Germany. That is understood. But after all, it is the leaders of the country who determine policy, and it is always a simple matter to drag the people along, whether it is a democracy, or a fascist dictatorship, or a parliament, or a communist dictatorship. Voice or no voice, the people can always be brought to the bidding of the leaders. That is easy. All you have to do is to tell them they are being attacked, and denounce the pacifists for lack of patriotism and exposing the country to danger. It works the same in any country."

Contrary to Goering's pronouncement, the leaders of most other countries have vigorously denounced international conflict and, at least in some cases, done their best to prevent it.

"Every gun that is made, every warship launched, every rocket fired, signifies, in the final sense, a theft from those who hunger and are not fed, those who are cold and are not clothed."

—DWIGHT D. EISENHOWER

"I have seen war. I have seen war on land and sea. I have seen blood running from the wounded. I have seen the dead in the mud. I have seen cities destroyed. I have seen children starving. I have seen the agony of mothers and wives. I hate war."

—FRANKLIN DELANO
ROOSEVELT

"War is a series of catastrophes that results in victory."

—GEORGES CLEMENCEAU
(1841–1929)
was Prime minister of France
during World War I.

"There never was a good war or a bad peace."

—BENJAMIN FRANKLIN

"I know war as few other men now living know it, and nothing to me is more revolting. I have long advocated its complete abolition, as its very destructiveness on both friend and foe has rendered it useless as a method of settling international disputes."

—DOUGLAS MACARTHUR

"War would end if the dead could return."

—STANLEY BALDWIN

Nonetheless, many have argued that war is often a necessary prelude to peace. Others contend that the way to peace is to stop war. Depending on which side of this argument you come down on, the following will be of service.

"The purpose of all wars . . . is peace."

—St. Augustine

"War is a poor chisel to carve out tomorrow."

—Martin Luther King Jr.

"You are not going to get peace with millions of armed men. The chariot of peace cannot advance over a road littered with cannon."

—David Lloyd George

"War is an ugly thing but not the ugliest of things. The decayed and degraded state of moral and patriotic feeling which thinks that nothing is worth war is much worse."

—John Stuart Mill

"What difference does it make to the dead, the orphans, and the homeless whether the mad destruction is wrought under the name of totalitarianism or the holy name of liberty or democracy?"

—Mohandas Gandhi

"War may sometimes be a necessary evil. But no matter how necessary, it is always an evil, never a good."

—Jimmy Carter

"You cannot simultaneously prevent and prepare for war."

—Albert Einstein

"It is an unfortunate fact that we can secure peace only by preparing for war."

—John F. Kennedy
(1917–1963)
was thirty-fifth president of the United States. He was assassinated on November 22, 1963.

"There is nothing so likely to produce peace as to be well prepared to meet the enemy."

—George Washington

"We make war that we may live in peace."

—Aristotle

The twentieth century ushered in an age in which, for the first time in human history, questions of war and peace became literally questions about the survival of the human race. This has given a new urgency to the problem of war, but sadly we seem as far as ever from a solution. However, you can make others aware of the wisdom of our elders regarding the subject by citing to them some of these quotations:

"Ours is a world of nuclear giants and ethical infants. We know more about war than we know about peace, more about killing than we know about living. We have grasped the mystery of the atom and rejected the Sermon on the Mount."

—OMAR BRADLEY

"I know not with what weapons World War III will be fought, but World War IV will be fought with sticks and stones."

—ALBERT EINSTEIN

"War does not determine who is right—only who is left."

—BERTRAND RUSSELL

"Only the dead have seen the end of war."

—GEORGE SANTAYANA

"War, in one form or another, appeared with the first man. At the dawn of history, its morality was not questioned; it was simply a fact, like drought or disease—the manner in which tribes and then civilizations sought power and settled their differences."

—BARACK OBAMA

"You can no more win a war than you can win an earthquake."

—JEANETTE RANKIN
(1880–1973)
was the first woman elected to Congress. Out of her pacifist convictions, she opposed U.S. entry into both world wars.

"War is a cowardly escape from the problems of peace."

—THOMAS MANN

C oncerning the conduct of war itself, we have long passed the point where we can talk about a "civilized" way to conduct war. Modern wars are anything but civilized, so feel free to let this fact be known.

"In war, truth is the first casualty."
—AESCHYLUS

"In time of war the loudest patriots are the greatest profiteers."
—AUGUST BEBEL

"The object of war is not to die for your country, but to make the other bastard die for his."
—GEORGE PATTON (1885–1945) commanded the U.S. Third Army during the invasion of France in 1944 and was hailed as a war hero.

"It is well that war is so terrible, or we should grow too fond of it."
—ROBERT E. LEE

"War is hell!"
—WILLIAM TECUMSEH SHERMAN

"The art of war is simple enough. Find out where your enemy is. Get at him as soon as you can. Strike him as hard as you can, and keep moving on."
—ULYSSES S. GRANT

"In peace the sons bury their fathers, but in war the fathers bury their sons."

—CROESUS

"War is too serious a matter to entrust to military men."
—GEORGES CLEMENCEAU

In some distant future, perhaps humankind will have learned a better way of settling disputes aside from killing one another. Citizens of that age will look back in wonder at their barbaric past. You can raise a glass to that bloodless future and quote one of these.

"Peace is not the absence of war; it is a virtue, a state of mind, a disposition for benevolence, confidence, and justice."

—BARUCH SPINOZA (1632–1677) precursor of the Enlightenment, is noted as much for his scientific as for his philosophic investigations.

"In such a world of conflict, a world of victims and executioners, it is the job of thinking people not to be on the side of the executioners."

—ALBERT CAMUS

"Can anything be stupider than that a man has the right to kill me because he lives on the other side of the river and his ruler has a quarrel with mine, though I have not quarreled with him?"

—BLAISE PASCAL

"Sometime they'll give a war and nobody will come."

—CARL SANDBURG

HISTORY

Intellectuals are generally divided on the subject of history. Some argue that we can learn everything from it; others claim that it teaches us nothing. You don't necessarily have to choose sides in this argument, but you should have some ammunition to throw out to both camps.

"History is a guide to navigation in perilous times. History is who we are and why we are the way we are."

—DAVID C. MCCULLOUGH

"We learn from history that we learn nothing from history."

—GEORGE BERNARD SHAW

"What experience and history teach is this—that people and governments never have learned anything from history, or acted on principles."

—GEORG WILHELM FRIEDRICH HEGEL (1770–1831) was among the most important nineteenth-century philosophers, famous for his theory of dialectical change.

"I have but one lamp by which my feet are guided, and that is the lamp of experience. I know no way of judging of the future but by the past."

—EDWARD GIBBON

"History is more or less bunk. It's tradition. We don't want tradition. We want to live in the present and the only history that is worth a tinker's damn is the history we make today."

—HENRY FORD

"The past is always a rebuke to the present."

—ROBERT PENN WARREN

"If you would understand anything, observe its beginning and its development."

—ARISTOTLE

"One faces the future with one's past."

—PEARL S. BUCK (1892–1973) was a novelist who lived in China and was the first woman to be awarded the Nobel Prize, for her novel *The Good Earth*.

"History is merely a list of surprises. It can only prepare us to be surprised yet again."

—KURT VONNEGUT

P art of the confusion over the usefulness of studying the past arises from whether history represents actual events or if historians are simply making it up. In other words, is history real or is it myth? Are historians capable of objectivity? Or are they simply voicing their own collection of prejudices and preconceptions? If you want to enter this discussion, do so by quoting one of the following.

"Patriotism ruins history."
—JOHANN WOLFGANG VON GOETHE

"History will be kind to me for I intend to write it."
—WINSTON CHURCHILL

"History consists of a series of accumulated imaginative inventions."
—VOLTAIRE

"Clio, the muse of history, is as thoroughly infected with lies as a street whore with syphilis."

—ARTHUR SCHOPENHAUER

(1788–1860)

was a German philosopher whose thought was generally pessimistic.

"The historian must not try to know what is truth, if he values his honesty; for if he cares for his truths, he is certain to falsify his facts."

—HENRY ADAMS

"History is the most dangerous product evolved from the chemistry of the intellect . . . . History will justify anything. It teaches precisely nothing, for it contains everything and furnishes examples of everything."

—PAUL VALÉRY

"Historian: an unsuccessful novelist."

—H. L. MENCKEN

"History is not history unless it is the truth."

—ABRAHAM LINCOLN

"Who does not know that the first law of historical writing is the truth."

—CICERO

So history is truth, rumor, falsehood, invented, objective, and infected with lies. Truly, as the Muslim historian Ibn Khaldun wrote, "It should be known that history is a discipline that has a great number of approaches." One thing many agree on, though, is that it tends to repeat itself. You can sound like a knowledgeable historian if you can quote a sentiment like these:

"Those who cannot learn from history are doomed to repeat it."
—GEORGE SANTAYANA
(1863–1952)
was a Spanish philosopher and poet, best remembered for the above quotation.

"People are trapped in history, and history is trapped in them."
—JAMES BALDWIN

"The great eventful Present hides the Past; but through the din/ Of its loud life hints and echoes from the life behind steal in."
—JOHN GREENLEAF WHITTIER

"History is a vast early warning system."
—NORMAN COUSINS

"History repeats itself, first as tragedy, second as farce."
—KARL MARX

"History does not repeat itself. The historians repeat one another."

—MAX BEERBOHM

"Whoever wishes to foresee the future must consult the past; for human events ever resemble those of preceding times. This arises from the fact that they are produced by men who ever have been, and ever shall be, animated by the same passions, and thus they necessarily have the same results."

—NICCOLÒ MACHIAVELLI

(1469–1527)

an Italian philosopher, is sometimes called the first modern political thinker because of his masterwork, *The Prince*

"The past does not repeat itself, but it rhymes."

—MARK TWAIN

"Each time history repeats itself, the price goes up."

—AUTHOR UNKNOWN

I n Jane Austen's novel *Northanger Abbey*, Catherine Morland complains, "History, real solemn history, I cannot be interested in. . . . I read it a little as a duty; but it tells me nothing that does not either vex or weary me. The quarrels of popes and kings, with wars and pestilences in every page; the men all so good for nothing, and hardly any women at all—it is very tiresome." Sadly, this is the view of most people who have sat in a college history class on a warm summer's afternoon, listening to the professor drone on in a voice as gray and drab as himself. If the subject of history comes up and someone says, "Oh, I never was any good at history," quote one of the following.

"Few will have the greatness to bend history itself; but each of us can work to change a small portion of events, and in the total of all those acts will be written the history of this generation."

—ROBERT F. KENNEDY

"Historical awareness is a kind of resurrection."

—WILLIAM LEAST HEAT MOON

"History is a race between education and catastrophe."

—H. G. WELLS (1866–1946)
novelist, historian, political figure, was co-founder of the Fabian Society of socialists in England.

"Anybody can make history. Only a great man can write it."

—OSCAR WILDE

"Men make their own history, but they do not make it just as they please; they do not make it under circumstances chosen by themselves, but under circumstances directly found, given and transmitted from the past."

—KARL MARX (1818–1883)
the father of Communism, lived most of his life in London, where he researched his massive opus, *Capital*.

"History, despite its wrenching pain, cannot be unlived, but if faced with courage, need not be lived again."

—MAYA ANGELOU

"History does nothing; it does not possess immense riches, it does not fight battles. It is men, real, living, who do all this."

—KARL MARX

PART VI

PHILOSOPHY

"I love talking about nothing. It is the

only thing I know anything about."

—OSCAR WILDE

LOVE

"Love," as the writer George Jean Nathan observed, "is an emotion experienced by the many and enjoyed by the few." Perhaps its very elusiveness is what makes it so fascinating to us. Justice Potter Stewart once said of pornography, "I don't know how to define it, but I know what it is when I see it." Most of us could say the same thing about love: we don't have a succinct explanation of it, but we recognize it in others and in ourselves.

Intellectuals, who generally prefer to reduce emotions to definitions, have been as puzzled as everyone else over the years by the flitting spirit of love. You can emulate their approach to this complicated feeling by citing something like the following.

"Love must be as much a light as it is a flame."

—HENRY DAVID THOREAU

"The one thing we can never get enough of is love. And the one thing we never give enough of is love."

—HENRY MILLER (1891–1980) was an American novelist known for his sexually explicit stories that were to some degree autobiographically based.

"If love is the answer, could you rephrase the question?"

—LILY TOMLIN

"For one human being to love another: that is perhaps the most difficult of our tasks; the ultimate, the last test and proof, the work for which all other work is but preparation."

—RAINER MARIA RILKE (1875–1926) a German-Austrian poet, had a profound influence on twentieth-century European literature.

"Love makes your soul crawl out from its hiding place."

—ZORA NEALE HURSTON

"Have you ever been in love? Horrible, isn't it? It makes you so vulnerable. It opens your chest and it opens your heart and it means someone can get inside you and mess you up. You build up all these defenses. You build up this whole armor, for years, so nothing can hurt you, then one stupid person, no different from any other stupid person, wanders into your stupid life . . . ."

—NEIL GAIMAN

"Love is the poetry of the senses."

—HONORÉ DE BALZAC

"Love is a condition in which the happiness of another person is essential to your own."

—ROBERT HEINLEIN

(1907–1988)

was among the most important science fiction authors of the twentieth century. His most widely read book is *Stranger in a Strange Land*.

Love can be so confusing that sometimes it's best treated with humor. In fact, sometimes that's the only way to approach it. Thus intellectuals prefer their love spiced with generous portions of cynicism. If you speak to a friend of love and want to appear detached and Olympian, consider making use of one of the following:

"Nothing takes the taste out of peanut butter quite like unrequited love."

—CHARLES SCHULZ (1922–2000)

one of the great cartoon geniuses of American literature, created the comic strip *Peanuts* in 1950.

"Oh, life is a glorious cycle of song,

A medley of extemporanea;

And love is a thing that can never go wrong;

And I am Marie of Romania."

—DOROTHY PARKER

"Love is the triumph of imagination over intelligence."

—H. L. MENCKEN

"Love is the delightful interval between meeting a beautiful girl and discovering that she looks like a haddock."

—JOHN BARRYMORE

"Before I met my husband, I'd never fallen in love, though I'd stepped in it a few times."

—RITA RUDNER

"Gravitation is not responsible for people falling in love."

—ALBERT EINSTEIN

Since love is so ineffable a quality, it's often easier to talk about the end of love or the lack of love. Plenty of people have found things to say about the tragedy of an old love affair or a failing marriage. You can sound both experienced and intellectual by quoting them.

"I hold it true, whate'er befall;

I feel it, when I sorry most;

'Tis better to have loved and lost

Than never to have loved at all."

—ALFRED, LORD TENNYSON
(1809–1892)
was the English Poet Laureate
during Victoria's reign.

"Love never dies a natural death. It dies because we don't know how to replenish its source. It dies of blindness and errors and betrayals. It dies of illness and wounds; it dies of weariness, of witherings, of tarnishings."

—ANAÏS NIN

"Love involves a peculiar unfathomable combination of understanding and misunderstanding."

—DIANE ARBUS (1923–1971) was a photographer whose works included *Identical Twins, Roselle, New Jersey, 1967*. She committed suicide at forty-eight.

"Friendship is the finest balm for the pangs of despised love."

—JANE AUSTEN

"You know you're in love when you don't want to fall asleep because reality is finally better than your dreams."

—THEODORE GEISEL (A.K.A. DR. SEUSS)

"Sometimes I wonder if men and women really suit each other. Perhaps they should live next door and just visit now and then."

—KATHARINE HEPBURN (1907–2003) was an American actress best known for her roles opposite Spencer Tracy in *Adam's Rib*, *Pat and Mike*, and others.

One of the peculiar features of love is that it doesn't just have to be between two people—though two is pretty much the minimum necessary. But love can be a transformative force in the world. If you want to say something lofty and socially conscious, employ something like these thoughts:

"Love is patient, love is kind. It does not envy, it does not boast, it is not proud. It is not rude, it is not self seeking. It is not easily angered, it keeps no record of wrongs. Love does not delight in evil but rejoices with the truth. It always protects, always trusts, always hopes, always perseveres. Love never fails."

—I CORINTHIANS 13:4–8

"Love is the only force capable of transforming an enemy into a friend."

—MARTIN LUTHER KING JR.

"Man has conquered whole nations, but all his armies could not conquer love. Man has chained and fettered the spirit, but he has been utterly helpless before love. . . Thus love has the magic power to make of a beggar a king. Yes, love is free; it can dwell in no other atmosphere."

—EMMA GOLDMAN (1869–1940) was an anarchist and political activist and advocate of birth control.

"Hatred ever kills, love never dies. Such is the vast difference between the two. What is obtained by love is retained for all time. What is obtained by hatred proves a burden in reality for it increases hatred."

—MOHANDAS GANDHI

"For there is one thing I can safely say: that those bound by love but obey each other if they are to keep company long. Love will not be constrained by master; when mastery comes, the God of love at once beats his wings and farewell he is gone."

—GEOFFREY CHAUCER

"Neither a lofty degree of intelligence nor imagination nor both together go to the making of genius. Love, love, love, that is the soul of genius."

—WOLFGANG AMADEUS MOZART

In the end, love is sitting with someone at the end of the day, watching the sun set, and knowing that even when neither of you is saying anything, the conversation between you will never end. That's the best kind of love. And here are some thoughts to help it along.

"I love you not only for what you are but for what I am when I am with you. I love you not only for what you have made of yourself but for what you are making of me. I love you for the part of me that you bring out."

—ELIZABETH BARRETT BROWNING (1806–1861) has been celebrated both for her poetry, such as *Sonnets from the Portuguese*, and for her marriage to the poet Robert Browning,

"That Love is all there is,

Is all we know of Love."

—EMILY DICKINSON

"He is not a lover who does not love forever."

—EURIPIDES

"Love at first sight is easy to understand; it's when two people have been looking at each other for a lifetime that it becomes a miracle."

—AMY BLOOM

"Love does not consist of gazing at each other, but in looking together in the same direction."

—ANTOINE DE SAINT-EXUPÉRY

"The first duty of love is to listen."

—PAUL TILLICH

"Love is a canvas furnished by Nature and embroidered by imagination."

—VOLTAIRE

"Those who love deeply never grow old; they may die of old age, but they die young."

—SIR ARTHUR PINERO

(1855–1944)

was an English actor and director. He was associated with Henry Irving's Lyceum Theater, as well as the Haymarket Theater in London.

"Keep love in your heart. A life without it is like a sunless garden when the flowers are dead. The consciousness of loving and being loved brings a warmth and richness to life that nothing else can bring."

—OSCAR WILDE

"Life is the flower for which love is the honey."

—VICTOR HUGO

MARRIAGE

Coming as it does after the lofty heights of love, marriage inevitably seems like a descent into something more mundane. Sometimes the decline is gentle and both participants have a chance to get used to breathing the thicker air in the lower altitudes of everyday life together. Sometimes it's more precipitate. And occasionally (the Paul McCartney-Heather Mills wedlock springs to mind), it's like falling off a cliff onto a bed of nails. Whatever the case, there's no lack of cynical comparisons between love and marriage. You can sound properly detached and disillusioned (two qualities essential to intellectualism) by quoting along the following lines:

"Getting married is a lot like getting into a tub of hot water. After you get used to it, it ain't so hot."

—MINNIE PEARL

"Marriage: A word which should be pronounced 'mirage.'"

—HERBERT SPENCER
(1820–1903)
English philosopher, is credited with the phrase "survival of the fittest" and with the creation of the philosophy of Social Darwinism.

"Bachelors know more about women than married men; if they didn't they'd be married too."

—H. L. MENCKEN

"The secret of a happy marriage remains a secret."

—HENNY YOUNGMAN

"Marriage, a market which has nothing free but the entrance."

—MICHEL DE MONTAIGNE

"Bride, n. A woman with a fine prospect of happiness behind her."

—AMBROSE BIERCE

"He that hath a wife and children hath given hostages to fortune."

—FRANCIS BACON

"It is not a lack of love, but a lack of friendship that makes unhappy marriages."

—FRIEDRICH NIETZSCHE

THE QUOTABLE INTELLECTUAL

"If you want to sacrifice the admiration of many men for the criticism of one, go ahead, get married."

—KATHARINE HEPBURN

"When two people are under the influence of the most violent, most insane, most delusive, and most transient of passions, they are required to swear that they will remain in that excited, abnormal, and exhausting condition continuously until death do them part."

—GEORGE BERNARD SHAW

"Any intelligent woman who reads the marriage contract, and then goes into it, deserves all the consequences."

—ISADORA DUNCAN (1877–1927) dancer, was widely hailed for her innovative and sensual style, considered by many a precursor to modern dance.

"Marriage, n. The state or condition of a community consisting of a master, a mistress and two slaves, making in all, two."

—AMBROSE BIERCE

M arriage has often been compared to war. The American humorist James Thurber captured this in cartoons (*The War Between Men and Women*). Others have said much the same thing over the centuries. These days wars are fought with bombs, bullets, and IEDs. Sometimes it seems as if the modern marriage is fought with lawyers, prenups, and depositions. If you and your spouse are deep in a discussion of your marriage and things seem to be growing tense, defuse the situation with an apt quotation.

"Marriage is the only war in which you sleep with the enemy."

—FRANÇOIS DE LA ROCHEFOUCAULD

"Marriage must constantly fight against a monster which devours everything: routine."

—HONORÉ DE BALZAC

"Never go to bed mad. Stay up and fight."

—Phyllis Diller

"Though women are angels, yet wedlock's the devil."

—Lord Byron

"I have yet to hear a man ask for advice on how to combine marriage and a career."

—Gloria Steinem

"All married couples should learn the art of battle as they should learn the art of making love. Good battle is objective and honest—never vicious or cruel. Good battle is healthy and constructive, and brings to a marriage the principle of equal partnership."

—Ann Landers

"My husband and I have never considered divorce . . . murder sometimes, but never divorce."

—Dr. Joyce Brothers

"Marriage is the alliance of two people, one of whom never remembers birthdays and the other who never forgets."

—Ogden Nash

"Marriage is an alliance entered into by a man who can't sleep with the window shut, and a woman who can't sleep with the window open."

—George Bernard Shaw

"How can a woman be expected to be happy with a man who insists on treating her as if she were a perfectly normal human being?"

—Oscar Wilde

"Though marriage makes man and wife one flesh, it leaves 'em still two fools."

—William Congreve

"So heavy is the chain of wedlock that it needs two to carry it, and sometimes three."

—Alexandre Dumas, fils

"The problem with marriage is that it ends every night after making love, and it must be rebuilt every morning before breakfast."

—GABRIEL GARCÍA MÁRQUEZ

(1927–)

Colombian novelist, most well-known for his book, *One Hundred Years of Solitude.*

"It destroys one's nerves to be amiable every day to the same human being."

—BENJAMIN DISRAELI

"In the early years, you fight because you don't understand each other. In the later years, you fight because you do."

—JOAN DIDION

"Strike an average between what a woman thinks of her husband a month before she marries him and what she thinks of him a year afterward, and you will have the truth about him."

—H. L. MENCKEN

"Why does a woman work ten years to change a man's habits and then complain that he's not the man she married?"

—BARBRA STREISAND

"No man is regular in his attendance at the House of Commons until he is married."

—BENJAMIN DISRAELI

Marriage, as any number of people have observed, is something that needs work. If you're wondering the best way of arriving at a peaceful old age in the company of your spouse, you might want to consider this advice.

"I have learned that only two things are necessary to keep one's wife happy. First, let her think she's having her own way. And second, let her have it."

—LYNDON B. JOHNSON

"My mother said it was simple to keep a man. You must be a maid in the living room, a cook in the kitchen, and a whore in the bedroom. I said I'd hire the other two and take care of the bedroom bit."

—JERRY HALL

"Once a woman has forgiven her man, she must not reheat his sins for breakfast."

—MARLENE DIETRICH

"Never strike your wife—even with a flower."

—HINDU PROVERB

"My wife tells me she doesn't care what I do when I'm away, as long as I'm not enjoying it."

—LEE TREVINO

"To keep your marriage brimming,

With love in the loving cup,

Whenever you're wrong, admit it;

Whenever you're right, shut up."

—OGDEN NASH

Still, not everyone scoffs at marriage. For some, it's the highest, truest, and best expression of love. When you're looking for something to write on that twenty-fifth anniversary card—the one standing next to the dozen roses, the bottle of champagne, and the two tickets to Paris—try one of these sentiments.

"If ever two were one, then surely we. If ever man were loved by wife, then thee."

—ANNE BRADSTREET

"Marriage is not a noun; it's a verb. It isn't something you get. It's something you do. It's the way you love your partner every day."

—BARBARA DE ANGELIS

"An ideal wife is any woman who has an ideal husband."

—BOOTH TARKINGTON

(1869–1946)

author of a number of popular novels, is remembered for *The Magnificent Ambersons* and for his Penrod stories.

"A good marriage is that in which each appoints the other guardian of his solitude."

—RAINER MARIA RILKE

"I think men who have a pierced ear are better prepared for marriage. They've experienced pain and bought jewelry."

—RITA RUDNER

"Chains do not hold a marriage together. It is threads, hundreds of tiny threads which sew people together through the years. That is what makes a marriage last— more than passion or even sex!"

—SIMONE SIGNORET

"The sum which two married people owe to one another defies calculation. It is an infinite debt, which can only be discharged through eternity."

—JOHANN WOLFGANG VON GOETHE

"No man or woman really knows what perfect love is until they have been married a quarter of a century."

—MARK TWAIN

"Here's to matrimony, the high sea for which no compass has yet been invented!"

—HEINRICH HEINE

"A happy marriage is a long conversation which always seems too short."

—ANDRÉ MAUROIS

"I love being married. It's so great to find that one special person you want to annoy for the rest of your life."

—RITA RUDNER

"One of the good things that come of a true marriage is, that there is one face on which changes come without your seeing them; or rather there is one face which you can still see the same, through all the shadows which years have gathered upon it."

—GEORGE MACDONALD
(1824–1905)
English author of fantasy novels, was a great influence on later authors such as J. R. R. Tolkien and C. S. Lewis.

"That quiet mutual gaze of a trusting husband and wife is like the first moment of rest or refuge from a great weariness or a great danger."

—GEORGE ELIOT

"There is no more lovely, friendly and charming relationship, communion or company than a good marriage."

—MARTIN LUTHER

The most profound and succinct comment on marriage comes to us, as does so much wisdom, from ancient Rome:

"And when will there be an end of marrying? I suppose, when there is an end of living!"

—TERTULLIAN

FRIENDSHIP

Ralph Waldo Emerson, the Sage of Concord, said, "The ornament of a house is the friends who frequent it." Like many men and women of culture, Emerson had a good deal to say about friends. In fact, from the beginnings of civilization people have tried to understand how to make friends, keep friends, and get rid of unwanted friends. Perhaps you're looking for something to write in a birthday card for one of your oldest friends. Consider one of these.

"Friendship makes prosperity more shining and lessens adversity by dividing and sharing it."
—CICERO

"What is a friend? A single soul dwelling in two bodies."
—ARISTOTLE

"True friendship consists not in the multitude of friends but in their worth and value."
—BEN JONSON (1572–1637) dramatist and actor, was a contemporary of William Shakespeare. His plays include *Vulpone* and *The Alchemist*.

"Friendship with oneself is all important because without it one cannot be friends with anybody else in the world."
—ELEANOR ROOSEVELT

"Perhaps the most delightful friendships are those in which there is much agreement, much disputation, and yet more personal liking."
—GEORGE ELIOT

"True friendship can afford true knowledge. It does not depend on darkness and ignorance."
—HENRY DAVID THOREAU

"Though friendship is not quick to burn,

It is explosive stuff."
—MAY SARTON (1912–1995) novelist, poet, and autobiographer whose writing was strongly influenced by her lesbian relationships.

"It is one of the blessings of old friends that you can afford to be stupid with them."

—RALPH WALDO EMERSON

(1803–1882)

a close friend of Thoreau, had a unifying effect on the New England-based movement that came to be known as Transcendentalism.

"We are all travelers in the wilderness of this world, and the best we can find in our travels is an honest friend."

—ROBERT LOUIS STEVENSON

"But friendship is precious, not only in the shade but in the sunshine of life; and thanks to a benevolent arrangement of things, the greater part of life is sunshine."

—THOMAS JEFFERSON

"It seems to me that trying to live without friends is like milking a bear to get cream for your morning coffee. It is a whole lot of trouble, and then not worth much after you get it."

—ZORA NEALE HURSTON

(1891–1960)

author and poet during the Harlem Renaissance, played a significant role in reviving African American folklore.

"Think where man's glory most begins and ends,

And say my glory was I had such friends."

—WILLIAM BUTLER YEATS

"Love is like the wild-rose briar;

Friendship is like the holly tree.

The holly is dark when the rose briar blooms,

But which will bloom most constantly?"

—EMILY BRONTË (1818–1848)

one of several highly talented members of the Yorkshire Brontë family, authored the Gothic classic *Wuthering Heights*.

A lot of time and effort has been expended on trying to find a surefire formula for making friends. No one's ever found a way that works every time, but it must be admitted that some people seem to be more successful at it than others. When the topic comes up during dinner table conversation, drop in something like this.

"You can make more friends in two months by becoming interested in other people than you can in two years by trying to get other people interested in you."

—DALE CARNEGIE

"Be courteous to all, but intimate with few, and let those few be well tried before you give them your confidence. True friendship is a plant of slow growth and must undergo and withstand the shocks of adversity before it is entitled to the appellation."

—GEORGE WASHINGTON

"We secure our friends not by accepting favors but by doing them."

—THUCYDIDES

"Friendship is born at that moment when one person says to another: 'What! You, too? Thought I was the only one.'"

—C. S. LEWIS

"The best time to make friends is before you need them."

—ETHEL BARRYMORE
(1879–1959)
member of the famous Barrymore acting family, won an Academy Award for Best Supporting Actress for *None but the Lonely Heart*.

"Choose your friends carefully. Your enemies will choose you."

—YASSIR ARAFAT

"It is in the thirties that we want friends. In the forties we know they won't save us any more than love did."

—F. SCOTT FITZGERALD

"The wicked can have only accomplices, the voluptuous have companions in debauchery, self-seekers have associates, the politic assemble the factions, the typical idler has connections, princes have courtiers. Only the virtuous have friends."

—VOLTAIRE

The truest test of friendship, of course, is how much your friends will tolerate you talking about yourself. Narcissism is probably the greatest enemy real friendship ever has. Still another test is your willingness to be honest with friends and their openness with you. If, however, you don't want to be open and wish to deflect the conversation, quote from one of these as a distraction from a deeper discussion of your feelings

"A man must eat a peck of salt with his friend before he knows him."

—Miguel de Cervantes

"Do not use a hatchet to remove a fly from your friend's forehead."

—Chinese proverb

"Only your real friends will tell you when your face is dirty."

—Sicilian proverb

"Men kick friendship around like a football, but it doesn't seem to crack. Women treat it like glass and it goes to pieces."

—Anne Morrow Lindbergh
(1906–2001)
the wife of aviator Charles Lindbergh, won fame in her own right as an author and early female aviator.

"Consult your friend on all things, especially on those which respect yourself. His counsel may then be useful where your own self-love might impair your judgment."

—Seneca

"The holy passion of friendship is so sweet and steady and loyal and enduring in nature that it will last through a whole lifetime, if not asked to lend money."

—Mark Twain

"True friendship can afford true knowledge. It does not depend on darkness and ignorance."

—Henry David Thoreau

"It is difficult to say who do you the most mischief: enemies with the worst intentions or friends with the best."

—Edward Bulwer-Lytton

"It is one of the severest tests of friendship to tell your friend his faults. So to love a man that you cannot bear to see a stain upon him and to speak painful truth through loving words, that is friendship."

—HENRY WARD BEECHER

(1813–1887)
associated with various radical causes of the Victorian era, including female suffrage, temperance, and evolution.

"The best way to destroy an enemy is to make him a friend."

—ABRAHAM LINCOLN

"Don't believe your friends when they ask you to be honest with them. All they really want is to be maintained in the good opinion they have of themselves."

—ALBERT CAMUS

"It's a lot like nature. You only have as many animals as the ecosystem can support and you only have as many friends as you can tolerate the bitching of."

—RANDY K. MILHOLLAND

"A true friend stabs you in the front."

—OSCAR WILDE

"Don't flatter yourself that friendship authorizes you to say disagreeable things to your intimates. The nearer you come into relation with a person, the more necessary do tact and courtesy become."

—OLIVER WENDELL HOLMES JR.

(1841–1935)
was a member of the United States Supreme Court for almost thirty years.

"Misfortune shows those who are not really friends."

—ARISTOTLE

"Between friends differences in taste or opinion are irritating in direct proportion to their triviality."

—W. H. AUDEN

"A good friend can tell you what is the matter with you in a minute. He may not seem such a good friend after telling."

—ARTHUR BRISBANE

"Prosperity makes friends, adversity tries them."

—PUBLILIUS SYRUS

(1ST CENTURY BCE)
is known for his epigrams, though his sole surviving work, *Sententiae*, may not even have been compiled by him.

Above all, friends are those people who stand by you no matter what. As movie diva Marlene Dietrich said, "It's the friends you can call up at four A.M. that matter." How many of us have friends like that? Make a list and send them a note with something from the following:

"The friendship that can cease has never been real."

—SAINT JEROME

"Perhaps the most delightful friendships are those in which there is much agreement, much disputation, and yet more personal liking."

—GEORGE ELIOT

"Let us be grateful to people who make us happy; they are the charming gardeners who make our souls blossom."

—MARCEL PROUST

"Some people go to priests; others to poetry; I to my friends."

—VIRGINIA WOOLF

"But if the while I think on thee, dear friend,

All losses are restored and sorrows end."

—WILLIAM SHAKESPEARE

"We are all travelers in the wilderness of this world, and the best we can find in our travels is an honest friend."

—ROBERT LOUIS STEVENSON

"Friendship is the only cement that will ever hold the world together."

—WOODROW WILSON

"In everyone's life, at some time, our inner fire goes out. It is then burst into flame by an encounter with another human being. We should all be thankful for those people who rekindle the inner spirit."

—ALBERT SCHWEITZER

"Constant use will not wear ragged the fabric of friendship."

—DOROTHY PARKER
(1893–1967)
poet and short story writer, was part of the circle of writers, actors, and literary figures known as the Algonquin Round Table

"The bird a nest, the spider a web, man friendship."

—WILLIAM BLAKE

"Friendship is a sheltering tree."

—SAMUEL TAYLOR COLERIDGE

"The language of friendship is not words but meanings."

—HENRY DAVID THOREAU

(1817–1862) best remembered for his book, *Walden*, an account of his life in a cabin by the shores of Walden Pond in Concord, Massachusetts.

"I am speaking now of the highest duty we owe our friends, the noblest, the most sacred—that of keeping their own nobleness, goodness, pure and incorrupt. If we let our friend become cold and selfish and exacting without a remonstrance, we are no true lover, no true friend."

—HARRIET BEECHER STOWE

"One friend in a lifetime is much; two are many; three are hardly possible."

—HENRY ADAMS

The Roman politician Cicero, who devoted an entire book to the subject of friendship, put it best:

"Life is nothing without friendship."

—CICERO

KNOWLEDGE

A little learning may be a dangerous thing, as the poet Alexander Pope observed, but the general consensus of intellectuals seems to be that too much learning can crush knowledge. Knowledge, as distinct from learning, is desirable, with wisdom being valued above either commodity. To appear wise as well as learned, feel free to use some of what follows in conversation.

"All men, by nature, desire knowledge."

—ARISTOTLE

"I am not young enough to know everything."

—OSCAR WILDE

"All wish to possess knowledge, but few, comparatively speaking, are willing to pay the price."

—JUVENAL (C. 60–C. 140)
a Roman poet, was the author of the *Satires*, a collection of poems that critiqued contemporary Roman society and customs.

"The good life is inspired by love and guided by knowledge."

—BERTRAND RUSSELL

"We can understand almost anything, but we can't understand how we understand."

—ALBERT EINSTEIN

"The beginning of knowledge is the discovery of something we do not understand."

—FRANK HERBERT

"Science is organized knowledge. Wisdom is organized life."

—IMMANUEL KANT

"If knowledge can create problems, it is not through ignorance that we can solve them."

—ISAAC ASIMOV

THE QUOTABLE INTELLECTUAL

"Knowledge will forever govern ignorance; and a people who mean to be their own governors must arm themselves with the power which knowledge gives."

—JAMES MADISON (1751–1836)

the fourth president of the United States, also played a central role in shaping the new republic by his role in the Constitutional Convention.

"The improvement of understanding is for two ends: first, our own increase of knowledge; secondly, to enable us to deliver that knowledge to others."

—JOHN LOCKE

"Great are they who see that spiritual is stronger than any material force, that thoughts rule the world."

—RALPH WALDO EMERSON

"There is much pleasure to be gained from useless knowledge."

—BERTRAND RUSSELL

"If you have knowledge, let others light their candles at it."

—MARGARET FULLER

(1810–1850)

a journalist and critic, was a close associate of Emerson and Thoreau and the Concord circle of thinkers.

"Knowledge and timber shouldn't be much used till they are seasoned."

—OLIVER WENDELL HOLMES

"Knowledge is power."

—FRANCIS BACON

"It is no good to try to stop knowledge from going forward. Ignorance is never better than knowledge."

—ENRICO FERMI

"Knowledge is not simply another commodity. On the contrary. Knowledge is never used up. It increases by diffusion and grows by dispersion."

—DANIEL BOORSTIN

(1914–2004)

historian, author of several works of popular history, was Librarian of the U.S. Congress for more than a decade.

"The only good is knowledge, and the only evil is ignorance."

—SOCRATES

Socrates' sentiment is all well and good, but how does one set about gaining knowledge? The first step, most authorities agree, is to accept your own ignorance. Humility isn't something that comes easily to intellectuals, but you can at least show you understand the need for its appearance by eating these slices of humble pie.

"To be conscious that you are ignorant is a great step to knowledge."

—BENJAMIN DISRAELI

"The dumbest people I know are those who know it all."

—MALCOLM FORBES

"Trust yourself. You know more than you think you do."

—BENJAMIN SPOCK

"Nothing that is worth knowing can be taught."

—OSCAR WILDE

"A man's errors are his portals of discovery."

—JAMES JOYCE (1882–1941) in such novels as *Ulysses* initiated a new style of writing, sometimes dubbed "stream of consciousness."

"It is impossible for a man to learn what he thinks he already knows."

—EPICTETUS

"Whosoever wishes to know about the world must learn about it in its particular details. Knowledge is not intelligence. In searching for the truth be ready for the unexpected."

—HERACLITUS (535 BCE–475 BCE) believed that the universe was in a constant state of flux. He also suggested that Logos (or "reason") governs all things.

"The eye sees only what the mind is prepared to comprehend."

—HENRI BERGSON

"Trust your hunches. They're usually based on facts filed away just below the conscious level."

—DR. JOYCE BROTHERS

"Each excellent thing, once learned, serves for a measure of all other knowledge."

—PHILIP SIDNEY

"Anyone who conducts an argument by appealing to authority is not using his intelligence; he is just using his memory."

—LEONARDO DA VINCI

"A great many people think they are thinking when they are merely rearranging their prejudices."

—WILLIAM JAMES

"Expertise in one field does not carry over into other fields. But experts often think so. The narrower their field of knowledge the more likely they are to think so."

—ROBERT HEINLEIN

"Integrity without knowledge is weak and useless, and knowledge without integrity is dangerous and dreadful."

—SAMUEL JOHNSON

"The fact that some geniuses were laughed at does not imply that all who are laughed at are geniuses. They laughed at Columbus, they laughed at Fulton, they laughed at the Wright brothers. But they also laughed at Bozo the Clown."

—CARL SAGAN

"When a true genius appears in the world you may know him by this sign: that all the dunces are in confederacy against him."

—JONATHAN SWIFT (1667–1745) wrote *Gulliver's Travels*, a commentary on the state of society in his day, as well as other satiric works.

"To succeed in the world it is not enough to be stupid, you must also be well-mannered."

—VOLTAIRE

"Knowledge is of two kinds: we know a subject ourselves, or we know where we can find information upon it."

—SAMUEL JOHNSON

"It is a great nuisance that knowledge can only be acquired by hard work."

—W. SOMERSET MAUGHAM

Knowledge is just the beginning, though. Intellectuals strive for wisdom, which means, essentially, admitting that the more they know, the more they know that they don't know. Furthermore, knowledge and wisdom can't be compelled and can't be controlled. Should the conversation take a turn in this direction, make sure your dinner guests know where you stand on the issue.

"An ounce of love is worth a pound of knowledge."

—JOHN WESLEY

"If we value the pursuit of knowledge, we must be free to follow wherever that search may lead us. The free mind is not a barking dog, to be tethered on a ten-foot chain."

—ADLAI STEVENSON (1900–1965) twice the unsuccessful candidate of the Democratic Party for president, was beloved of liberals for his intellect and brilliant speeches.

"If you don't read the newspaper, you are uninformed; if you do read the newspaper, you are misinformed."

—MARK TWAIN

"Bodily exercise, when compulsory, does no harm to the body; but knowledge which is acquired under compulsion obtains no hold on the mind."

—PLATO

"Whoever undertakes to set himself up as a judge of Truth and Knowledge is shipwrecked by the laughter of the gods."

—ALBERT EINSTEIN

"There is no squabbling so violent as that between people who accepted an idea yesterday and those who will accept the same idea tomorrow."

—CHRISTOPHER MORLEY

"Perplexity is the beginning of knowledge."

—KAHLIL GIBRAN (1883–1931) a Lebanese-American poet, is best remembered for *The Prophet*, a collection of essays that surged in popularity during the 1960s.

"Knowledge comes, but wisdom lingers."

—ALFRED, LORD TENNYSON

"Knowledge is of no value unless you put it into practice."

—ANTON CHEKOV

"Those that know, do. Those that understand, teach."

—ARISTOTLE

"Be wiser than other people if you can, but do not tell them so."

—LORD CHESTERFIELD

"Knowing others is wisdom; knowing yourself is Enlightenment."

—LAO TZU

"Let us be thankful for the fools. But for them the rest of us could not succeed."

—MARK TWAIN (1835–1910) whose real name was Samuel L. Clemens, authored such classics as *Tom Sawyer* and *Huckleberry Finn*.

"The more I know,

the less tortured

I am."

—ALANIS MORISSETTE

POWER

Knowledge may be power, but it doesn't follow that the reverse is true. Power is often in the hands of the ignorant, something that causes intellectuals to sit up late at night drinking too much white wine, gobbling Brie, and worrying about the state of the world. It may be that you can offer some comfort with words of great thinkers. It may not make anyone feel more powerful, but it should at least make them feel as if wisdom is in their corner.

"No science is immune to the infection of politics and the corruption of power."

—JACOB BRONOWSKI

"Power tends to corrupt, and absolute power corrupts absolutely."

—LORD ACTON

"Power corrupts the few, while weakness corrupts the many."

—ERIC HOFFER

"The highest proof of virtue is to possess boundless power without abusing it."

—LORD MACAULAY

"Power has only one duty—to secure the social welfare of the People."

—BENJAMIN DISRAELI

"I hope our wisdom will grow with our power, and teach us, that the less we use our power the greater it will be."

—THOMAS JEFFERSON
(1743–1826)
author of the Declaration of Independence and founder of the University of Virginia, was the third president of the United States.

"We look forward to the time when the Power of Love will replace the Love of Power. Then will our world know the blessings of peace."

—WILLIAM GLADSTONE

"Concentrated power has always been the enemy of liberty."
—RONALD REAGAN

"Arbitrary power is most easily established on the ruins of liberty abused to licentiousness."
—GEORGE WASHINGTON

"There is no knowledge that is not power."
—RALPH WALDO EMERSON

"Who is wise? He that learns from everyone. Who is powerful? He that governs his passions. Who is rich? He who is content. Who is that? Nobody."
—BENJAMIN FRANKLIN
(1706–1790)
scientist and inventor, was a printer and a writer, as well as a politician and diplomat.

"Justice without force is powerless; force without justice is tyrannical."
—BLAISE PASCAL

"There will be no end to the troubles of states, or of humanity itself, till philosophers become kings in this world, or till those we now call kings and rulers really and truly become philosophers, and political power and philosophy thus come into the same hands."
—PLATO

The chief power one can hold, so voices from the past tell us, is power over oneself. That may be comforting in a world in which the powerful are increasingly uncaring about the powerless. At least there's something we can accomplish.

"He is the most powerful who has power over himself."
—SENECA

"He who controls others may be powerful, but he who has mastered himself is mightier still."
—LAO TZU
(C. 604 BCE–C. 531 BCE)
is revered as a god in the Taoist religion, which is largely based on his teachings of self-discipline and mysticism.

"The power of man has grown in every sphere except over himself."
—WINSTON CHURCHILL

"The love of liberty is the love of others; the love of power is the love of ourselves."
—WILLIAM HAZLITT

"Nearly all men can stand adversity, but if you want to test a man's character, give him power."

—ABRAHAM LINCOLN

"To achieve, you need thought. You have to know what you are doing and that's real power."

—AYN RAND (1905–1982)
is known for her novels *The Fountainhead* and *Atlas Shrugged*, which expounded her philosophy of enlightened self-interest.

"The attempt to combine wisdom and power has only rarely been successful and then only for a short while."

—ALBERT EINSTEIN

P ower, according to most intellectuals' way of thinking, is exercised by the wise person over herself and by the ignorant over others (most notoriously in the world of the intellectual it is exercised by university administrators over professors). By its nature it is corrupting and evil. The advantage of this point of view is that it allows you to feel superior to those who are oppressing you. If that's the case, keep some of these sentiments handy.

"Power is given only to those who dare to lower themselves and pick it up."

—FYODOR DOSTOEVSKY

"Power, like a desolating pestilence,

Pollutes whate'er it touches."

—PERCY SHELLEY

"In order to obtain and hold power, a man must love it."

—LEO TOLSTOY

"Arbitrary power is like most other things which are very hard—very liable to be broken."

—ABIGAIL ADAMS

"What we call Man's power over Nature turns out to be a power exercised by some men over other men with Nature as its instrument."

—C. S. LEWIS (1898–1963) medievalist and the author of the *Narnia* children's fantasy series, was a powerful defender of Christian theology.

"Power is something of which I am convinced there is no innocence this side of the womb."

—NADINE GORDIMER

"Once you give a charlatan power over you, you almost never get it back."

—CARL SAGAN

"Never work just for money or for power. They won't save your soul or help you sleep at night."

—MARION WRIGHT EDELMAN

P ower, as numerous thinkers have reminded us, doesn't give itself away. It has to be taken; often the seizure of power is by those on whose behalf it was supposedly being exercised. If you want to show yourself as a champion of the oppressed against their oppressors, launch one of these quotations into the conversation.

"Power concedes nothing without a demand. It never did, and it never will."

—FREDERICK DOUGLASS

"Power can be taken, but not given. The process of the taking is empowerment in itself."

—GLORIA STEINEM (1934–) founder of *Ms.* magazine. She led campaigns for abortion rights, culminating in the 1973 Supreme Court decision *Roe v. Wade*.

"Free election of masters does not abolish the masters or the slaves."

—HERBERT MARCUSE

"You can have power over people as long as you don't take everything away from them. But when you've robbed a man of everything, he's no longer in your power."

—ALEKSANDR SOLZHENITSYN

"Of all tyrannies, a tyranny exercised for the good of its victims may be the most oppressive."

—C. S. LEWIS

"Where justice is denied, where poverty is enforced, where ignorance prevails, and where any one class is made to feel that society is an organized conspiracy to oppress, rob, and degrade them, neither persons nor property will be safe."

—FREDERICK DOUGLASS

"The most common way people give up their power is by thinking they don't have any."

—ALICE WALKER

There's something very attractive about power. Even if we don't have it, we seem drawn to it. So perhaps the best thing is to admit we find it fascinating—after all, so many interesting people, for good or for ill, have had it.

"God is on everyone's side . . . and in the last analysis, he is on the side with plenty of money and large armies."

—JEAN ANOUILH (1910–1987)
French dramatist, is best known in the United States as the author of *Becket or The Honor of God.*

"All too often arrogance accompanies strength, and we must never assume that justice is on the side of the strong. The use of power must always be accompanied by moral choice."

—THEODORE BIKEL

"Power is when you have every justification to kill someone and then you don't."

—OSKAR SCHINDLER

"I am not interested in power for power's sake but I'm interested in power that is moral, that is right, and that is good."

—MARTIN LUTHER KING JR.

"Power is my mistress. I have worked too hard at her conquest to allow anyone to take her away from me."

—NAPOLEON BONAPARTE
(1769–1821)
rose from the rank of corporal in the French army to become emperor of France.

"The world itself is the will to power—and nothing else! And you yourself are the will to power—and nothing else!"

—FRIEDRICH NIETZSCHE

"Silence is the ultimate weapon of power."

—CHARLES DE GAULLE

"Being powerful is like being a lady. If you have to tell people you are, you aren't."

—MARGARET THATCHER

"You see what power is—holding someone else's fear in your hand and showing it to them!"

—AMY TAN (1952–)
has turned her experiences as a Chinese American into themes for such novels as *The Joy Luck Club* and *The Kitchen God's Wife*.

"The great secret of power is never to will to do more than you can accomplish."

—HENRIK IBSEN

"The problem of power is how to achieve its responsible use rather than its irresponsible and indulgent use—of how to get men of power to live for the public rather than off the public."

—ROBERT F. KENNEDY

"Power is the ultimate aphrodisiac."

—HENRY KISSINGER (1923–)
served in the Nixon administration, first as national security advisor, then as secretary of state.

"Power consists in one's capacity to link his will with the purpose of others, to lead by reason and a gift of cooperation."

—WOODROW WILSON

"I love power. But it is as an artist that I love it. I love it as a musician loves his violin, to draw out its sounds and chords and harmonies."

—NAPOLEON BONAPARTE

"Power in America today is control of the means of communication."

—THEODORE WHITE

"The first principle of a civilized state is that power is legitimate only when it is under contract."

—WALTER LIPPMANN

"The illegal we do immediately, the unconstitutional takes a little longer."

—HENRY KISSINGER

OLD AGE

The book of Ecclesiastes says, "Again I saw that under the sun the race is not to the swift, nor the battle to the strong, nor bread to the wise, nor riches to the intelligent, nor favor to those with knowledge, but time and chance happen to them all."

Time, indeed, comes to all of us. Our hair thins, our skin wrinkles, our steps grow slower, and we climb stairs at a gentler pace. Old age is to be celebrated as a time of wisdom and experience, or—particularly if you're under thirty—feared as the demon waiting hidden around the corner. Fortunately, as you grow older you acquire a rich stock of quotes with which to counter the protestations of the young.

"If you live to be one hundred, you've got it made. Very few people die past that age."

—GEORGE BURNS

"The tragedy of old age is not that one is old but that one is young."

—OSCAR WILDE

"No man loves life like him that's growing old."

—SOCRATES

"Forty is the old age of youth; fifty the youth of old age."

—VICTOR HUGO

"The old are in a second childhood."

—AESCHYLUS (525 BCE–426 BCE)

early Greek playwright, was noted for his tragedies, including *The Oresteia*, *Seven Against Thebes*, and *The Suppliant*s.

"Grow old along with me!

The best is yet to be,

The last of life, for which the first was made."

—ROBERT BROWNING

"I think your whole life shows in your face and you should be proud of that."
—LAUREN BACALL

"Old age is like everything else. To make a success of it, you've got to start young."
—THEODORE ROOSEVELT

"I want to die young at a ripe old age."
—ASHLEY MONTAGU
(1905–1999)
anthropologist and humanist scholar, is the author of a number of works dealing with the need for racial tolerance.

"Age is something that doesn't matter, unless you are a cheese."
—BILLIE BURKE

"First you are young; then you are middle-aged; then you are old; then you are wonderful."
—LADY DIANA COOPER

"The great thing about getting older is that you don't lose all the other ages you've been."
—MADELEINE L'ENGLE

"Old age is the most unexpected of all the things that can happen to a man."
—LEON TROTSKY

One's attitude to old age depends largely on whether one accepts it or wrestles with it. On the whole, it's probably better to accept its inevitability, since it's a wrestling match you're sure to lose. There's plenty of wisdom on both sides of the question.

"To get back my youth I would do anything in the world, except take exercise, get up early, or be respectable."
—OSCAR WILDE

"I don't believe one grows older. I think that what happens early on in life is that at a certain age one stands still and stagnates."
—T. S. ELIOT (1888–1965)
was a poet whose works were influential in developing Modernism.

"How pleasant is the day when we give up striving to be young— or slender."
—WILLIAM JAMES

"It takes a long time to become young."
—PABLO PICASSO

THE QUOTABLE INTELLECTUAL

"Growing old is a bad habit which a busy man has no time to form."

—ANDRÉ MAUROIS

"Age is an issue of mind over matter. If you don't mind, it doesn't matter."

—MARK TWAIN

"When grace is joined with wrinkles, it is adorable. There is an unspeakable dawn in happy old age."

—VICTOR HUGO

"A man is not old until regrets take the place of dreams."

—JOHN BARRYMORE

"Old age adds to the respect due to virtue, but it takes nothing from the contempt inspired by vice; it whitens only the hair."

—IRA GERSHWIN (1896–1983) together with his brother George, wrote many acclaimed Broadway shows and movies, including *Porgy and Bess* and *An American in Paris*.

"There is more felicity on the far side of baldness than young men can possibly imagine."

—LOGAN PEARSALL SMITH

"It's sad to grow old, but nice to ripen."

—BRIGITTE BARDOT

"A man's only as old as the woman he feels."

—GROUCHO MARX

"I don't plan to grow old gracefully. I plan to have face lifts until my ears meet."

—RITA RUDNER

Some people greet old age like a valued companion, while for others it's only a harbinger of inevitable and painful decay. For many, the onset of old age is accompanied by such stages as denial, bargaining, anger, and, finally, acceptance. Depending on which of those stages you're in will determine which of the following quotes you choose to unleash into a gathering of intellectuals who are trying to stare down middle age.

"As I give thought to the matter, I find four causes for the apparent misery of old age: first, it withdraws us from active accomplishments; second, it renders the body less powerful; third, it deprives us of almost all forms of enjoyment; fourth, it stands not far from death."

—CICERO

"A woman has the age she deserves."

—COCO CHANEL

"Every old man complains of the growing depravity of the world, of the petulance and insolence of the rising generation."

—SAMUEL JOHNSON

"There's no such thing as old age, there is only sorrow."

—EDITH WHARTON (1862–1937)
prolific novelist and interior designer, wrote such important books as *Ethan Frome* and *The House of Mirth*.

"The older I grow, the more I distrust the familiar doctrine that age brings wisdom."

—H. L. MENCKEN

"What is the worst of woes that wait on age?

What stamps the wrinkle deeper on the brow?

To view each loved one blotted from life's page,

And be alone on earth, as I am now."

—LORD BYRON

"Age is a very high price to pay for maturity."

—TOM STOPPARD

"Whatever poet, orator, or sage may say of it, old age is still old age."

—SINCLAIR LEWIS

Still, taken all around, there are certainly worse things than old age. And if someone you know has been complaining a lot about their aches and pains, comfort them with this.

"Old age isn't so bad when you consider the alternative."

—MAURICE CHEVALIER

"I'm very pleased to be here. Let's face it, at my age I'm very pleased to be anywhere."

—GEORGE BURNS (1896–1996) vaudeville, film, and television actor, continued working until the very end of his life at age 100.

"Sex at the age of eighty-four is a wonderful experience. Especially the one in the winter."

—MILTON BERLE

"The old begin to complain of the conduct of the young when they themselves are no longer able to set a bad example."

—FRANÇOIS DE LA ROCHEFOUCAULD

"The youth gets together his materials to build a bridge to the moon, or, perchance, a palace or temple on the earth, and, at length, the middle-aged man concludes to build a woodshed with them."

—HENRY DAVID THOREAU

"The great secret that all old people share is that you really haven't changed in seventy or eighty years. Your body changes, but you don't change at all. And that, of course, causes great confusion."

—DORIS LESSING (1919–) is the British author of such notable novels as *The Golden Notebook* and *The Good Terrorist*.

"I recently had my annual physical examination, which I get once every seven years, and when the nurse weighed me, I was shocked to discover how much stronger the Earth's gravitational pull has become since 1990."

—DAVE BARRY

"Regrets are the natural property of grey hairs."

—CHARLES DICKENS

"Life is a moderately good play with a badly written third act."

—TRUMAN CAPOTE

"An aged man is but a paltry thing,

A tattered coat upon a stick, unless

Soul clasp its hands and sing, and louder sing

For every tatter in its mortal dress."

—WILLIAM BUTLER YEATS
(1865–1939)
one of Ireland's most important twentieth-century poets, was deeply involved in the Irish literary revival at the beginning of the century.

"All diseases run into one—old age."

—RALPH WALDO EMERSON

"The first forty years of life give us the text; the next thirty supply the commentary on it."

—ARTHUR SCHOPENHAUER

"Life would be infinitely happier if we could only be born at the age of eighty and gradually approach eighteen."

—MARK TWAIN

"Advice in old age is foolish; for what can be more absurd than to increase our provisions for the road the nearer we approach to our journey's end."

—CICERO

"In old age we are like a batch of letters that someone has sent. We are no longer in the past, we have arrived."

—KNUT HAMSUN

MONEY

Money is something most intellectuals hold in contempt. This is because most of them don't have it, would like to have it, but don't want to admit wanting to have it. In fact, in the circles in which the true cognoscenti move, it is considered declassé to do anything for money. Instead there should be a "higher calling" of some kind—from God, society, the *New York Times* editorial page . . . whatever.

Intellectuals enjoy tossing off quotations about the absurdity of money—that it won't buy happiness, is the root of all evil, and so forth. It's best to do this in the presence of someone who has a great deal of money. For example, if you find yourself at a party in a Park Avenue apartment and the person next to you has taken a sip of Dom Pérignon from his cut-glass champagne flute while casually mentioning that he and his partner are wintering in the south of France this year on his yacht, you can let drop one of the following:

"The chief value of money lies in the fact that one lives in a world in which it is overestimated."

—H. L. MENCKEN

"Money often costs too much."

—RALPH WALDO EMERSON

"Endless money forms the sinews of war."

—CICERO (106 BCE–43 BCE) wrote Latin literature that is considered by many the apex of the Golden Age of Roman prose.

"Money is like manure, of very little use except to be spread."

—FRANCIS BACON

"Money is not required to buy one the necessity of the soul."

—HENRY DAVID THOREAU

"A wise man should have money in his head but not in his heart."

—JONATHAN SWIFT

"If money help a man to do good to others, it is of some value; but if not, it is simply a mass of evil, and the sooner it is got rid of, the better."

—SWAMI VIVEKENANDA

"It's the wretchedness of being rich that you have to live with rich people."

—LOGAN PEARSALL SMITH

"Too many of us look upon Americans as dollar chasers. This is a cruel libel, even if it is reiterated thoughtlessly by the Americans themselves."

—ALBERT EINSTEIN

"I choose the likely man in preference to the rich man. I want a man without money rather than money without a man."

—THEMISTOCLES (524 BCE–459 BCE)
played a major role in Athens' nascent democracy. He was a commander at the battle of Marathon in 490 BCE.

"If you want to know what God thinks of money, look at the people he gave it to."

—DOROTHY PARKER

Of course, when pushed on the point, intellectuals will admit that money is necessary. Not for them, of course, they hasten to add. But Ordinary People need it to get by. Thus, while idly turning the pages of the *New Yorker* or *The Nation* or flipping through channels to find the local PBS station, you can casually observe:

"Money isn't everything. But lack of money isn't anything."

—GEORGE S. KAUFMANN

"Money is like a sixth sense, and you can't make use of the other five without it."

—W. SOMERSET MAUGHAM

"Money can't buy friends, but it can get you a better class of enemy."

—SPIKE MILLIGAN (1918–2002)
was a comedian and creator of *The Goon Show*, a pioneering British comedy series of the 1940s and 1950s.

"He that is of the opinion money will do everything may well be suspected of doing everything for money."

—BENJAMIN FRANKLIN

"If you can count your money, you don't have a billion dollars."

—J. PAUL GETTY

"Be rich to yourself and poor to your friends."

—JUVENAL

"It is better to have a permanent income than to be fascinating."

—OSCAR WILDE

"I'd like to live as a poor man with lots of money."

—PABLO PICASSO

"A rich man is nothing but a poor man with money."

—W. C. FIELDS (1880–1946)
was one of the great comedians of early American film.

"Money is better than poverty, if only for financial reasons."

—WOODY ALLEN

"The only way not to think of money is to have a great deal of it."

—EDITH WHARTON

"You can be young without money. But you can't be old without it."

—TENNESSEE WILLIAMS

"Lack of money is the root of all evil."

—GEORGE BERNARD SHAW

In the recent past, money has been much in the news, particularly as invested in banks and the stock market. Banks and bankers are a bit like lawyers—always a good subject for snarky quotations. Try some of these on your friends in the financial industry.

"A banker is a fellow who lends you his umbrella when the sun is shining but wants it back the minute it begins to rain."

—MARK TWAIN

"The concerned investment banker is the one who blows the horn on his Mercedes as he drives through a red light."

—ANONYMOUS

"It is easier to rob by setting up a bank than by holding up a bank clerk."

—BERTOLT BRECHT (1898–1956)
German poet and playwright, is best known for his musical play (cowritten with Kurt Weil) *The Threepenny Opera*.

"Because bankers measure their self-worth in money, and pay themselves a lot of it, they think they're fine fellows and don't need to explain themselves."

—JOHN BUCHAN

"I believe that banking institutions are more dangerous to our liberties than standing armies."

—THOMAS JEFFERSON

Finally, of course, should the subject of your own income come up in conversation, it's best to turn it into a joke while at the same time making it clear that money is something you never think about, save in jest.

"My problem lies in reconciling my gross habits with my net income."

—ERROL FLYNN

"Money frees you from doing things you dislike. Since I dislike doing nearly everything, money is handy."

—GROUCHO MARX

"I have enough money to last me the rest of my life, unless I buy something."

—JACKIE MASON

SEX

Dorothy Parker once arrived at a Halloween party. "Come on in," the host said. "We're ducking for apples."

"Change one letter in that last sentence," muttered Mrs. Parker, "and you have the story of my life."

Intellectual attitudes toward sex are complicated. On the one hand, those who live the life of the mind have needs and drives like everyone else. On the other hand, they're rather embarrassed by them. For an intellectual, talking about sex is a bit like reaching for a well-thumbed copy of Marcus Aurelius's *Meditations* and discovering to his horror that he's picked up the *Sports Illustrated* swimsuit issue by mistake.

Therefore, the best way to approach the delicate topic of male-female relations in the bedroom is to make light of it, commenting over the wine and canapés with something along the following lines:

"Don't knock masturbation—it's sex with someone I love."

—WOODY ALLEN

"Sex. In America an obsession. In other parts of the world a fact."

—MARLENE DIETRICH

"Love is the answer, but while you are waiting for the answer, sex raises some pretty good questions."

—WOODY ALLEN

"Life without sex might be safer but it would be unbearably dull."

—H. L. MENCKEN

"Sex: the thing that takes up the least amount of time and causes the most amount of trouble."

—JOHN BARRYMORE
(1882–1942)

among the most charismatic and talented of the Barrymore family of actors, was noted for his portrayal of Richard III.

"Love ain't nothing but sex misspelled."

—HARLAN ELLISON

"When the authorities warn you of the dangers of having sex, there is an important lesson to be learned. Do not have sex with the authorities."

—MATT GROENING

"The tragedy is when you've got sex in the head instead of down where it belongs."

—D. H. LAWRENCE

"I believe that sex is a beautiful thing between two people. Between five, it's fantastic."

—WOODY ALLEN

"I think people should be free to engage in any sexual practices they choose; they should draw the line at goats, though."

—ELTON JOHN

"Nothing risqué, nothing gained."

—ALEXANDER WOOLLCOTT

(1887–1943)

was a leading New York theater critic.

"Sex is one of the most wholesome, beautiful, and natural experiences that money can buy."

—STEVE MARTIN

"**D**o you find it easy to get drunk on words," asks a character in Dorothy Sayers's novel *Gaudy Night*. "So much so," replies her companion, "that I am scarcely ever perfectly sober." Words can entice as easily as wine, and if conversation turns to the art of seduction, you can offer plenty of advice from the following.

"For women the best aphrodisiacs are words. The G-spot is in the ears. He who looks for it below there is wasting his time."

—ISABEL ALLENDE

"There are a number of mechanical devices which increase sexual arousal, particularly in women. Chief among these is the Mercedes-Benz 380SL convertible."

—P. J. O'ROURKE

"It's not true that I had nothing on. I had the radio on."

—MARILYN MONROE

"Christ died for our sins. Dare we make his martyrdom meaningless by not committing them?"

—JULES FEIFFER (1929–) is an American cartoonist and political activist, whose cartoons in the *Village Voice* won him a Pulitzer Prize.

"Graze on my lips; and if those hills be dry, stray lower, where the pleasant fountains lie."

—WILLIAM SHAKESPEARE

"Brevity is the soul of lingerie."

—DOROTHY PARKER

"Sex pleasure in woman is a kind of magic spell; it demands complete abandon; if words or movements oppose the magic of caresses, the spell is broken."

—SIMONE DE BEAUVOIR

"It's been so long since I made love I can't even remember who gets tied up."

—JOAN RIVERS

Sex is inextricably linked to two things far less romantic: marriage and children. If these come up, have something like the following handy:

"No matter how much cats fight, there always seem to be plenty of kittens."

—ABRAHAM LINCOLN

"Familiarity breeds contempt— and children."

—MARK TWAIN

"The reproduction of mankind is a great marvel and mystery. Had God consulted me in the matter, I should have advised him to continue the generation of the species by fashioning them out of clay."

—MARTIN LUTHER (1483–1546) was one of the originators of the Protestant Reformation and its most prominent spokesperson.

"The art of procreation and the members employed therein are so repulsive, that if it were not for the beauty of the faces and the adornments of the actors and the pent-up impulse, nature would lose the human species."

—LEONARDO DA VINCI

"You know, of course, that the Tasmanians, who never committed adultery, are now extinct."

—W. SOMERSET MAUGHAM

"I know nothing about sex because I was always married."

—ZSA ZSA GABOR

"The Love Bird is 100 percent faithful to his mate as long as they are locked in the same cage together."

—WILL CUPPY (1884–1949) was an American humorist whose best-known book is *The Decline and Fall of Practically Everybody*.

Should the subject of your own sex life come up, be prepared to pass it off lightly. There's nothing so boring to someone else than hearing about the great sex you're having with your boyfriend or girlfriend.

"If it wasn't for pickpockets and frisking at the airport, I'd have no sex life at all."
—RODNEY DANGERFIELD

"A terrible thing happened to me last night again—nothing."
—PHYLLIS DILLER

"Lead me not into temptation—I can find the way myself."
—RITA MAE BROWN

"Life is a sexually transmitted disease."

—R. D. LAING

"Sex," John Updike observed, "is like money; only too much is enough." It is perhaps not surprising that something necessary to the continuance of the human race preoccupies us so much. What is startling is the apparently excessive amount of time and effort it takes to get it right. In the following thoughts, you may find some helpful instruction—or at least something to show others that you know about the arts of love.

"When it comes to being a good lover, a guy has to ask a girl what she wants and be willing to give it to her."
—JENNA JAMESON

"Whoever called it necking was a poor judge of anatomy."
—GROUCHO MARX

"The difference between pornography and erotica is lighting."
—GLORIA LEONARD

"Sex is emotion in motion."

—MAE WEST (1893–1980)
one of film's earliest sex symbols, was wildly
bawdy in an age that tried to greatly restrict
such moments on the screen.

"Were kisses all the joys in bed

One woman would another wed."

—WILLIAM SHAKESPEARE

"We have reason to believe that man first walked upright to free his hands for masturbation."

—LILY TOMLIN

"Sexual intercourse is kicking death in the ass while singing."

—CHARLES BUKOWSKI
(1920–1994)
was an American poet and novelist. His works
concentrated on ordinary citizens and the
simple details of their lives.

"Men reach their sexual peak at eighteen. Women reach theirs at thirty-five. Do you get the feeling that God is playing a practical joke?"

—RITA RUDNER

JOHNNY AND FRANKIE WERE LOVERS.
OHO MY GOD..HOW THEY LOVED!
JOAN HELD,JR   (OLD SONG)

"There is nothing safe about sex. There never will be."

—NORMAN MAILER

"One half of the world cannot understand the pleasures of the other."

—JANE AUSTEN

"If sex is such a natural phenomenon, how come there are so many books on how to do it?"

—BETTE MIDLER

"Sex is one of the nine reasons for reincarnation—the other eight are unimportant."

—HENRY MILLER

"Sexuality is the lyricism of the masses."

—CHARLES BAUDELAIRE

"Sexual love is the most stupendous fact of the universe and the most magical mystery our poor blind senses know."

—AMY LOWELL

"Sex and beauty are inseparable, like life and consciousness."

—D. H. LAWRENCE (1885–1930) novelist and essayist, probed areas of human sexual relationships, defying many of the early publishing taboos on the subject.

"Sex lies at the root of life, and we can never learn to reverence life until we know how to understand sex."

—HENRY ELLIS

"Instruction in sex is as important as instruction in food; yet not only are our adolescents not taught the physiology of sex, but never warned that the strongest sexual attraction may exist between persons so incompatible in tastes and capacities that they could not endure living together for a week much less a lifetime."

—GEORGE BERNARD SHAW

The point of sex—which sometimes people need to be reminded of—is to enjoy it. And there's nothing wrong with a laugh or two along the way. If things seem to be getting too serious in the bedroom, take out one of these and improve the mood.

"From the moment I was six, I felt sexy. And let me tell you, it was hell, sheer hell, waiting to do something about it."
—BETTE DAVIS

"I used to be Snow White, but I drifted."
—MAE WEST

"The ability to make love frivolously is the chief characteristic which distinguishes human beings from the beasts."
—HEYWOOD BROUN

"To err is human, but it feels divine."
—MAE WEST

"Some things are better than sex, and some are worse, but there's nothing exactly like it."
—W. C. FIELDS

"Sex appeal is 50 percent what you've got and 50 percent what people think you've got."

—Sophia Loren

"Sex is as important as eating or drinking and we ought to allow the one appetite to be satisfied with as little restraint or false modesty as the other."

—Marquis de Sade
(1740–1814)

whose name gave us Sadism, was a French aristocrat and author whose books dealt in detail with his sexual conquests.

"Sex contains all, bodies, souls,

Meanings, proofs, purities, delicacies, results, promulgations,

All hopes, benefactions, bestowals, all the passions, loves, beauties, delights of the earth,

All the governments, judges, gods."

—Walt Whitman

EDUCATION

Intellectuals, with a few exceptions, agree that education is important. However, most of them don't think that their schooling played a large role in educating them, and they're divided on whether schools should be improved or simply abolished. They admire teachers in general but seem to dislike those particular teachers who taught them, since they claim it takes years to undo the effects of poor instruction in the classroom. No matter what your educational background and experiences, be prepared to toss out something like these to show you recognize the inadequacy of formal education.

"A mind is a fire to be kindled, not a vessel to be filled."
—PLUTARCH

"It is, in fact, nothing short of a miracle that the modern methods of instruction have not entirely strangled the holy curiosity of inquiry."
—ALBERT EINSTEIN

"Nine tenths of education is encouragement."
—ANATOLE FRANCE

"Education is the transmission of civilization."
—WILL AND ARIEL DURANT

"Education is the best provision for old age."
—ARISTOTLE

"A well-informed mind is the best security against the contagion of folly and of vice."
—ANN RADCLIFFE (1764–1823) author of early Gothic novels, is best known for *The Mysteries of Udolpho* and *The Italian*.

"Only the educated are free."
—EPICTETUS

"Perhaps the most valuable result of all education is the ability to make yourself do the thing you have to do, when it ought to be done, whether you like it or not."
—THOMAS HUXLEY

"The highest result of education is tolerance."
—HELEN KELLER

"Education's purpose is to replace an empty mind with an open one."

—Malcolm S. Forbes

There are also those who claim education is a harmful activity, tampering with a more virtuous ignorance or with knowledge derived from outside the confines of the classroom. "Ignorance," Oscar Wilde remarked, "is like a delicate exotic fruit; touch it and the bloom is gone." You can imply the uselessness of all educational systems while at the same time showing your own sophistication and erudition by casually lobbing a quotation such as the following into a conversation about learning.

"What does education often do? It makes a straight-cut ditch of a free, meandering brook."

—HENRY DAVID THOREAU

"Education: the inculcation of the incomprehensible into the indifferent by the incompetent."

—JOHN MAYNARD KEYNES

"Education is what remains when we have forgotten all that we have been taught."

—GEORGE SAVILE (1633–1695) was a leader of England's Glorious Revolution, which deposed James II and replaced him with William of Orange and his queen, Mary.

"Education . . . has produced a vast population able to read but unable to distinguish what is worth reading."

—G. M. TREVELYAN

"Thank goodness I was never sent to school. It would have rubbed off some of the originality."

—BEATRIX POTTER

"College isn't the place to go for ideas."

—HELEN KELLER

"A university is what a college becomes when the faculty loses interest in students."

—JOHN CIARDI

"Don't set your wit against a child."

—JONATHAN SWIFT

"In the first place God made idiots. This was for practice. Then He made School Boards."

—MARK TWAIN

"Fathers send their sons to college either because they went to college or because they didn't."

—L. L. HENDERSON

"The advantage of a classical education is that it enables you to despise the wealth that it prevents you from achieving."

—RUSSELL GREEN

"It is a thousand times better to have common sense without education than to have education without common sense.

—ROBERT G. INGERSOLL (1833–1899) was an outstanding freethinker, who defended the philosophic position of agnosticism.

"There is nothing so stupid as the educated man if you get him off the thing he was educated in."

—WILL ROGERS

"I have never let my schooling interfere with my education."

—MARK TWAIN

"I prefer the company of peasants because they have not been educated sufficiently to reason incorrectly."

—MICHEL DE MONTAIGNE

The purpose of education is to fill the empty vessel of the mind, to make students better, more productive members of society, to teach social responsibility, or to do all and none of these things. Any one of the following should be useful in the event that your friends start chatting about teachers and education.

"Everyone has a right to a university degree in America, even if it's in Hamburger Technology."

—CLIVE JAMES (1939–)
is a television personality in England and in Australia.

"The foundation of every state is the education of its youth."

—DIOGENES LAERTIUS

"The direction in which education starts a man will determine his future life."

—PLATO

"If you think education is expensive, try ignorance."

—DEREK CURTIS BOK

"Education is the ability to listen to almost anything without losing your temper or your self-confidence."

—ROBERT FROST

"Any genuine teaching will result, if successful, in someone's knowing how to bring about a better condition of things than existed earlier."

—JOHN DEWEY (1859–1952) was the chief representative of pragmatic philosophy in America and a leader of the progressive education movement.

"Education is the transmission of civilization."

—WILL AND ARIEL DURANT

"That is what learning is. You suddenly understand something you've understood all your life, but in a new way."

—DORIS LESSING

"In a completely rational society, the best of us would aspire to be teachers and the rest of us would have to settle for something less, because passing civilization along from one generation to the next ought to be the highest honor and the highest responsibility anyone could have."

—LEE IACOCCA

"It must be remembered that the purpose of education is not to fill the minds of students with facts . . . it is to teach them to think, if that is possible, and always to think for themselves."

—ROBERT HUTCHINS

"The job of an educator is to teach students to see vitality in themselves."

—JOSEPH CAMPBELL

"Every time you stop a school, you will have to build a jail. What you gain at one end you lose at the other. It's like feeding a dog on his own tail. It won't fatten the dog."

—MARK TWAIN

"Learning is a treasure that will follow its owner everywhere."

—CHINESE PROVERB

"Education is not preparation for life; education is life itself."

—JOHN DEWEY

"The true teacher defends his pupils against his own personal influence."

—A. BRONSON ALCOTT

FAME

Fame is deplored largely by those who are famous, much as money is held in contempt by those who have a lot of it. We are living in a time when the definition of "famous" has extended from people who've actually done something to people who are famous for being underwear-challenged, such as Paris Hilton or Britney Spears. Probably the most quoted comment about fame is Andy Warhol's "In the future everyone will be world-famous for fifteen minutes." It's instructive to keep an eye on the tabloid pages to determine who's on their fourteenth minute.

Before the latter half of the twentieth century, fame was something people worked to acquire, though they often pretended not to. Today, when it seems everyone is striving to be on Reality TV, you can display your contempt for such vulgar ambitions by quoting something like this:

"Fame is the thirst of youth."

—LORD BYRON

"The strongest poison ever known came from Caesar's laurel crown."

—WILLIAM BLAKE (1757–1827) was a poet, painter, and printmaker, who unified all these talents to create a strange cycle of myth, poetry, and art.

"True glory takes root and even spreads; all false pretences, like flowers, fall to the ground; nor can any counterfeit last long."

—CICERO

"Worldly fame is but a breath of wind that blows now this way, and now that, and changes name as it changes direction."

—DANTE ALIGHIERI

"He that pursues fame with just claims, trusts his happiness to the winds; but he that endeavors after it by false merit, has to fear, not only the violence of the storm, but the leaks of his vessel."

—SAMUEL JOHNSON

"The fame of great men ought to be judged always by the means they used to acquire it."

—FRANÇOIS DE LA ROCHEFOUCAULD

"True glory consists in doing what deserves to be written; in writing what deserves to be read; and in so living as to make the world happier and better for our living in it."

—PLINY THE ELDER

"Fame has also this great drawback, that if we pursue it, we must direct our lives so as to please the fancy of men."

—BARUCH SPINOZA

"Fame is no plant that grows on mortal soil."

—JOHN MILTON (1608–1674) is considered by many to be England's greatest poet outside of Shakespeare. His masterwork is the epic poem *Paradise Lost*.

"Fame and power are the objects of all men. Even their partial fruition is gained by very few; and that, too, at the expense of social pleasure, health, conscience, life."

—BENJAMIN DISRAELI

"What is popularly called fame is nothing but an empty name and a legacy from paganism."

—DESIDERIUS ERASMUS

"All the fame you should look for in life is to have lived it quietly."

—MICHEL DE MONTAIGNE

"Fame is like a river, that beareth up things light and swollen, and drowns things weighty and solid."

—FRANCIS BACON

"All is ephemeral—fame and the famous as well."

—MARCUS AURELIUS

"Fame is a fickle food

Upon a shifting plate."

—EMILY DICKINSON

"Fame is the perfume of heroic deeds."

—SOCRATES

"Fame and tranquility can never be bedfellows."

—MICHEL DE MONTAIGNE (1533–1592) popularized the essay (from the French "to try") as a literary form.

Gradually, fame has come to be seen as an end in itself, something decried by thinkers of the past but hailed by some of today's entertainers. The following quotations should be pitched in tones of contempt, showing that although the foolish may be seduced by the bubble reputation, you are above such fleeting things.

"Don't confuse fame with success. Madonna is one; Helen Keller is the other."

—ERMA BOMBECK

"I won't be happy till I'm as famous as God."

—MADONNA

"I want to be famous everywhere."

—LUCIANO PAVAROTTI

"The professional celebrity, male and female, is the crowning result of the star system of a society that makes a fetish of competition. In America, this system is carried to the point where a man who can knock a small white ball into a series of holes in the ground with more efficiency than anyone else thereby gains social access to the president of the United States."

—C. WRIGHT MILLS

"Fame is fickle and I know it. It has its compensations, but it also has its drawbacks, and I've experienced them both."

—MARILYN MONROE

(1926–1962)
showed her comedic abilities in Billy Wilder's *Some Like It Hot*. She was found dead in 1962, an apparent victim of a drug overdose.

"I'm shy, paranoid, whatever word you want to use. I hate fame. I've done everything I can to avoid it."

—JOHNNY DEPP

"Fame hit me like a ton of bricks."

—EMINEM

"Sometimes I wish I weren't famous."

—TAMMY WYNETTE

You can show your contempt for worldly fame by gently disparaging it while at the same time implying that if you were to get your fifteen minutes it would be for something worthwhile, like curing cancer or stopping world hunger.

"I'm afraid of losing my obscurity. Genuineness only thrives in the dark. Like celery."

—ALDOUS HUXLEY

"It is a short walk from the hallelujah to the hoot."

—VLADIMIR NABOKOV

"A celebrity is one who is known to many persons he is glad he doesn't know."

—H. L. MENCKEN

"The highest form of vanity is a love of fame."

—GEORGE SANTAYANA

"He lives in fame that died in virtue's cause."

—WILLIAM SHAKESPEARE

"The fact that my fifteen minutes of fame has extended a little longer than fifteen minutes is somewhat surprising to me and completely baffling to my wife."

—BARACK OBAMA

"The fame you earn has a different taste from the fame that is forced upon you."

—GLORIA VANDERBILT (1924–)
American heiress and socialite, was the subject of a conflict between her guardians, who sought to control her trust fund.

"It is strange to be known so universally and yet to be so lonely."

—ALBERT EINSTEIN

"Fame is proof that people are gullible."

—RALPH WALDO EMERSON

"I do not like the man who squanders life for fame; give me the man who living makes a name."

—EMILY DICKINSON

"Even those who write against fame wish for the fame of having written well, and those who read their works desire the fame of having read them."

—BLAISE PASCAL

"If you modestly enjoy your fame you are not unworthy to rank with the holy."

—Johann Wolfgang von Goethe (1749–1832) was a leader of the German Romantic movement in art and literature.

"The longer a man's fame is likely to last, the longer it will be in coming."

—Arthur Schopenhauer

"Good fame is like fire; when you have kindled you may easily preserve it; but if you extinguish it, you will not easily kindle it again."

—Francis Bacon

"Fame usually comes to those who are thinking about something else."

—Oliver Wendell Holmes

PART VII

NATURE

"Adopt the pace of nature.

Her secret is patience."

—RALPH WALDO EMERSON

NATURE

"Nature red in tooth and claw," wrote Alfred Lord Tennyson in the nineteenth century, citing the inexorable, merciless character of the natural world. Yet for centuries humans have respected and even worshipped nature. Today, many reject not only fur and sport hunting but renounce meat altogether in an effort to live at peace with plants and animals. It's not hard to see why: In a world filled with violence and horror, nature seems to offer a serene vista of harmony and peace. You too can draw and dispense inspiration from the words of those who adore nature as a friend and companion.

"The best remedy for those who are afraid, lonely or unhappy is to go outside, somewhere where they can be quiet, alone with the heavens, nature, and God. Because only then does one feel that all is as it should be and that God wishes to see people happy, amidst the simple beauty of nature."

—ANNE FRANK

"Nature is an infinite sphere of which the center is everywhere and the circumference nowhere."

—BLAISE PASCAL (1623–1662)
wrote on subjects ranging from geometry and probability theory to physics.

"My best Acquaintances are those

With whom I spoke no Word—

The Stars that stated come to Town

Esteemed Me never rude

Although to their Celestial Call

I failed to make reply—

My constant—reverential Face

Sufficient Courtesy."

—EMILY DICKINSON

"Study nature, love nature, stay close to nature. It will never fail you."

—FRANK LLOYD WRIGHT

"Those who contemplate the beauty of the earth find reserves of strength that will endure as long as life lasts."

—RACHEL CARSON (1907–1964) nature writer and marine biologist, exposed the damaging use of pesticides in her book *Silent Spring*.

"What humbugs we are, who pretend to live for Beauty, and never see the Dawn!"

—LOGAN PEARSALL SMITH

"When I go into the garden with a spade, and dig a bed, I feel such an exhilaration and health that I discover that I have been defrauding myself all this time in letting others do for me what I should have done with my own hands."

—RALPH WALDO EMERSON

"To see a world in a grain of sand,

And a heaven in a wild flower,

Hold infinity in the palm of your hand,

An eternity in an hour."

—WILLIAM BLAKE

"The goal of life is living in agreement with nature."

—ZENO

"To sit in the shade on a fine day and look upon verdure is the most perfect refreshment."

—JANE AUSTEN

"Look deep into nature, and then you will understand everything better."

—ALBERT EINSTEIN

"What would the world be, once bereft

Of wet and wildness? Let them be left,

O let them be left, wildness and wet,

Long live the weeds and the wildness yet."
—GERARD MANLEY HOPKINS
(1844–1889)
a leading Victorian poet, was much ahead of his time in his use of imagery.

"I'll tell you how the sun rose a ribbon at a time."
—EMILY DICKINSON

"Breathless, we flung us on a windy hill,

Laughed in the sun, and kissed the lovely grass."
—RUPERT BROOKE

"I am in love with the green earth."
—CHARLES LAMB

"The world will never starve for wonder but only for want of wonder."
—G. K. CHESTERTON

"I think it annoys God if you walk by the color purple in a field and don't notice."

—ALICE WALKER

W illiam Wordsworth, wandering lonely as a cloud, found his spirit renewed by a field of golden daffodils. He's by no means the first to discover beauty and wonder in flowers. If you send a bouquet to someone, accompany it with a sentiment.

"Flowers are heaven's masterpiece."

—DOROTHY PARKER

"The sun does not shine for a few trees and flowers but for the wide world's joy."

—HENRY WARD BEECHER

"The earth laughs in flowers."

—RALPH WALDO EMERSON

"Flowers are the sweetest things that God ever made and forgot to put a soul into."

—HENRY WADSWORTH LONG-

FELLOW (1807–1882)

wrote his poems on distinctively American themes, such as "Paul Revere's Ride" and "The Song of Hiawatha."

"A weed is no more than a flower in disguise."

—JAMES RUSSELL LOWELL

N ineteenth- and twentieth-century writers believed that nature was a guide to a higher purpose. It represented a divine order and beauty that can't be found in the works of Man. You can elevate the tone of any conversation about nature by quoting from the following.

"To me a lush carpet of pine needles or spongy grass is more welcome than the most luxurious Persian rug."

—HELEN KELLER

"Nature abhors a vacuum, and if I can only walk with sufficient carelessness I am sure to be filled."

—HENRY DAVID THOREAU

"I've made an odd discovery. Every time I talk to a savant I feel quite sure that happiness is no longer a possibility. Yet when I talk with my gardener, I'm convinced of the opposite."

—BERTRAND RUSSELL

"And how should a beautiful, ignorant stream of water know it heads for an early release— out across the desert, running toward the Gulf, below sea level, to murmur its lullaby, and see the Imperial Valley rise out of burning sand with cotton blossoms, wheat, watermelons, roses, how should it know?"

—CARL SANDBURG

"I will be the gladdest thing under the sun.

I will touch a hundred flowers and not pick one."

—EDNA ST. VINCENT MILLAY

(1892–1950)

was a poet and part of the Greenwich Village artistic scene in the 1930s and 1940s.

"People with a planet without flowers would think we must be mad with joy the whole time to have such things about us."

—IRIS MURDOCH

"I believe a leaf of grass is no less than the journey-work of the stars."

—WALT WHITMAN

"If a man walks in the woods for love of them half of each day, he is in danger of being regarded as a loafer. But if he spends his days as a speculator, shearing off those woods and making the earth bald before her time, he is deemed an industrious and enterprising citizen."

—HENRY DAVID THOREAU

"I love to think of nature as an unlimited broadcasting station, through which God speaks to us every hour, if we will only tune in."

—GEORGE WASHINGTON CARVER

N ature can be unforgiving as well as beautiful, and not all thoughts about her are benevolent. If you want to resist a close friend's suggestion that a brisk walk of ten miles through muddy fields in a driving rainstorm would be just the thing to get the blood circulating, try quoting from the following:

"Nature has no mercy at all. Nature says, 'I'm going to snow. If you have on a bikini and no snowshoes, that's tough. I am going to snow anyway.'"
—MAYA ANGELOU

"In nature there are neither rewards nor punishments. There are consequences."
—ROBERT G. INGERSOLL

"If people think nature is their friend, then they sure don't need an enemy."
—KURT VONNEGUT

"Adapt or perish, now as was ever, is nature's inexorable imperative."
—H. G. WELLS

M any have noted the close connection between Nature and Art. Indeed, for much of the nineteenth century artists and poets believed that true Art derived from Nature. Although nowadays intellectuals reject this as naïve and simplistic, you can still stir cocktail conversation with something along these lines:

"The poetry of the earth is never dead."
—JOHN KEATS (1795–1821)
had significant influence after his early death, though his poetry is more notable for what it might have become than for what it is.

"Keep your love of nature, for that is the true way to understand art more and more."
—VINCENT VAN GOGH

"Nature is a revelation of God; art is a revelation of man."
—HENRY WADSWORTH LONGELLOW

"To the artist there is never anything ugly in nature."

—AUGUST RODIN

"If nature were not beautiful, it would not be worth knowing, and if nature were not worth knowing, life would not be worth living."

—HENRI POINCARÉ

"Nature is beneficent. I praise her and all her works. She is silent and wise. She is cunning but for good ends. She has brought me here and will also lead me away."

—JOHANN WOLFGANG VON GOETHE

Above all, you can quote the wisdom of the past and present to impress upon your listeners the need to respect Nature and her close friendship with humans. If we don't destroy her, she has wonderful revelations for us.

"Man has been endowed with reason, with the power to create, so that he can add to what he's been given. But up to now he hasn't been a creator, only a destroyer. Forests keep disappearing, rivers dry up, wild life's become extinct, the climate's ruined and the land grows poorer and uglier every day."

—ANTON CHEKHOV

"We cannot command nature except by obeying her."

—FRANCIS BACON

"God writes the gospel not in the Bible alone, but on trees and flowers and clouds and stars."

—MARTIN LUTHER

"The sun, with all those plants revolving around it and dependent upon it, can still ripen a bunch of grapes as if it had nothing else in the universe to do."

—GALILEO GALILEI
(1564–1642)
was a scientist and a strong supporter of Copernicus's theory of a sun-centered planetary system.

"Forget not that the earth delights to feel your bare feet and the winds long to play with your hair."

—KAHLIL GIBRAN

"If one way be better than another, that you may be sure is Nature's way."

—ARISTOTLE

"There is not a sprig of grass that shoots uninteresting to me."

—THOMAS JEFFERSON

"Maybe nature is fundamentally ugly, chaotic, and complicated. But if it's like that, then I want out."

—STEVEN WEINBERG

"The day, water, sun, moon, night—I do not have to purchase these things with money."

—PLAUTUS

"The fog comes in on little cat feet. It sits looking over the harbor and city on silent haunches and then moves on."

—CARL SANDBURG

"Nature reserves the right to inflict upon her children the most terrifying jests."

—THORNTON WILDER

"Let us permit nature to have her way. She understands her business better than we do."

—MICHEL DE MONTAIGNE

ANIMALS

Mohandas Gandhi, among the great figures of twentieth-century national movements, once remarked, "The greatness of a nation and its moral progress can be judged by the way its animals are treated."

Humans love animals. They are affectionate, loyal, uncomplaining (mostly), and reliable. Yet throughout history, they've been mistreated, abused, and killed with no good reason. Animals serve to ground us and remind us of our place in the scheme of things. These words can do the same.

"I like pigs. Dogs look up to us. Cats look down on us. Pigs treat us as equals."
—WINSTON CHURCHILL

"Animals are such agreeable friends—they ask no questions, they pass no criticisms."
—GEORGE ELIOT

"Horse sense is the thing a horse has that keeps it from betting on people."
—W. C. FIELDS

"The bee is more honored than other animals, not because she labors but because she labors for others."
—ST. JOHN CHRYSOSTOM
(347–407)
an early father of the church, is honored as a saint by the Eastern Orthodox faith.

"Don't approach a goat from the front, a horse from the back, or a fool from any side."
—YIDDISH PROVERB

"Animals generally return the love you lavish on them by a swift bite in passing—not unlike friends and wives."
—GERALD DURRELL

"Life is as dear to a mute creature as it is to man. Just as one wants happiness and fears pain, just as one wants to live and not die, so do other creatures."

—DALAI LAMA

"Mankind's true moral test, its fundamental test (which lies deeply buried from view), consists of its attitude towards those who are at its mercy: animals. And in this respect mankind has suffered a fundamental debacle, a debacle so fundamental that all others stem from it."

—MILAN KUNDERA

"I don't believe in the concept of hell, but if I did I would think of it as filled with people who were cruel to animals."

—GARY LARSON

"A Robin Redbreast in a cage

Puts all Heaven in a Rage."

—WILLIAM BLAKE

"The indifference, callousness and contempt that so many people exhibit toward animals is evil first because it results in great suffering in animals, and second because it results in an incalculably great impoverishment of the human spirit."

—ASHLEY MONTAGU

"If you have men who will exclude any of God's creatures from the shelter of compassion and pity, you will have men who will deal likewise with their fellow men."

—ST. FRANCIS OF ASSISI
(1181–1226)
founder of the Franciscan order, dedicated his life to poverty and charity. He is the patron saint of animals.

"He who is cruel to animals becomes hard also in his dealings with men. We can judge the heart of a man by his treatment of animals."

—IMMANUEL KANT

"An animal's eyes have the power to speak a great language."

—MARTIN BUBER

Humans by and large tend to separate into two great groups: cat people and dog people. Depending on which group you fall into, you can use the following thoughts to propel conversation.

"Dogs come when they're called; cats take a message and get back to you later."

—MARY BLY

"A black cat crossing your path signifies that the animal is going somewhere."

—GROUCHO MARX

"The problem with cats is that they get the same exact look whether they see a moth or an ax murderer."

—PAULA POUNDSTONE

"Cats are connoisseurs of comfort."

—JAMES HERRIOTT (1916–1995) pen name of Alf Wight, a Yorkshire veterinarian whose memoir was published in the United States as *All Creatures Great and Small*.

"Never wear anything that panics the cat."

—P. J. O'ROURKE

"The great pleasure of a dog is that you may make a fool of yourself with him and not only will he not scold you, but he will make a fool of himself too."

—SAMUEL BUTLER

"Time spent with cats is never wasted."

—SIGMUND FREUD

"Dogs are getting bigger, according to a leading dog manufacturer."

—LEO ROSTEN

"The dog has got more fun out of Man than Man has got out of the dog, for the clearly demonstrable reason that Man is the more laughable of the two animals."

—JAMES THURBER

"You enter into a certain amount of madness when you marry a person with pets."

—NORA EPHRON (1941–) author and film director, has created a number of hit movies, including *Sleepless in Seattle*, *Julie and Julia*, and *When Harry Met Sally*.

The most basic point about animals and intellectuals is that the latter, except under extreme provocation, don't shoot or eat the former. Instead, intellectuals can be counted on to respect animals, sometimes to extremes. Quote something like this to them to make them feel better.

"Animals are my friends, and I don't eat my friends."

—GEORGE BERNARD SHAW

"Until one has loved an animal, a part of one's soul remains unawakened."

—ANATOLE FRANCE

"Any glimpse into the life of an animal quickens our own and makes it so much the larger and better in every way."

—JOHN MUIR

"Animals have these advantages over man: They have no theologians to instruct them, their funerals cost them nothing, and no one starts lawsuits over their wills."

—VOLTAIRE

"The animals of the world exist for their own reasons. They were not made for humans any more than black people were made for white, or women created for men."

—ALICE WALKER (1944–)
is an American author, best known for her novel *The Color Purple*, which was made into a hit film and for which she won a Pulitzer Prize.

"The best thing about animals is that they don't talk much."

—THORNTON WILDER

"Animals give me more pleasure through the viewfinder of a camera than they ever did in the crosshairs of a gunsight. And after I've finished 'shooting,' my unharmed victims are still around for others to enjoy. I have developed a deep respect for animals. I consider them fellow living creatures with certain rights that should not be violated any more than those of humans."

—JIMMY STEWART

"The squirrel that you kill in jest, dies in earnest."

—HENRY DAVID THOREAU

"I ask people why they have deer heads on their walls. They always say because it's such a beautiful animal. There you go. I think my mother is attractive, but I have photographs of her."

—ELLEN DEGENERES

"When a man wantonly destroys one of the works of man we call him a vandal. When he destroys one of the works of God we call him a sportsman."

—JOSEPH WOOD KRUTCH

"The fascination of shooting as a sport depends almost wholly on whether you are at the right or wrong end of a gun."

—P. G. WODEHOUSE (1881–1975) is best known as the creator of the comic duo Bertie Wooster and his valet Jeeves.

"A growing and increasingly influential movement of philosophers, ethicists, law professors, and activists are convinced that the great moral struggle of our time will be for the rights of animals."

—MICHAEL POLLAN

"To a man whose mind is free there is something even more intolerable in the sufferings of animals than in the sufferings of man. For with the latter it is at least admitted that suffering is evil and that the man who causes it is a criminal. But thousands of animals are uselessly butchered every day without a shadow of remorse. If any man were to refer to it, he would be thought ridiculous. And that is the unpardonable crime."

—ROMAIN ROLLAND

"All animals are equal, but some animals are more equal than others."

—GEORGE ORWELL

"If having a soul means being able to feel love and loyalty and gratitude, then animals are better off than a lot of humans."

—JAMES HERRIOTT

"It is just like man's vanity and impertinence to call an animal dumb because it is dumb to his dull perceptions."

—MARK TWAIN

"All of the animals except for man know that the principle business of life is to enjoy it."

—SAMUEL BUTLER

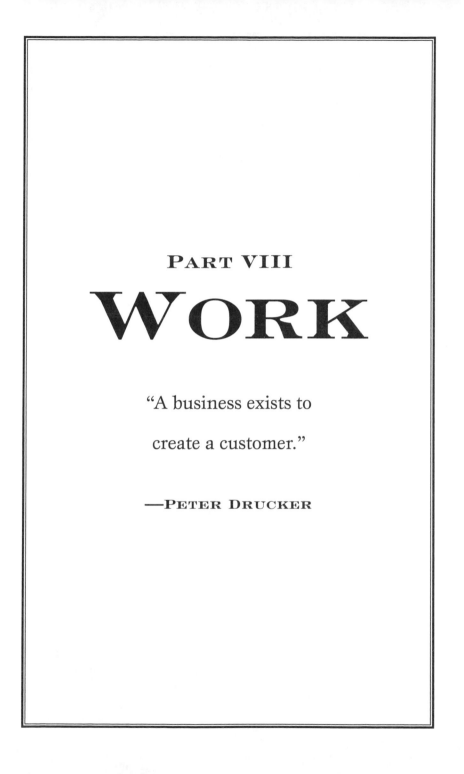

PART VIII

WORK

"A business exists to

create a customer."

—PETER DRUCKER

BUSINESS

President Calvin Coolidge remarked in the 1920s, "The business of America is business." Of course, since then we've had the Great Depression, one or two world wars, a couple of smaller wars, an extended economic boom, and the Great Recession, not to mention 9/11, disco, and the advent of reality TV. So it's possible that the business of America is a bit more complicated than Coolidge made it out to be.

Whatever the case, business has always been at the heart of American life and culture. If you want to sound informed, let off a quote from one of these.

"Whenever you see a successful business, someone once made a courageous decision."
—PETER DRUCKER

"The goal of war is peace, of business, leisure."
—ARISTOTLE

"No nation was ever ruined by trade."
—BENJAMIN FRANKLIN

"Business is a combination of war and sport."
—ANDRÉ MAUROIS

"Business, more than any other occupation, is a continual dealing with the future; it is a continual calculation, an instinctive exercise in foresight."
—HENRY R. LUCE (1898–1967)
founder of *Time* magazine and a powerful figure in the Republican Party and conservative politics.

"Every young man would do well to remember that all successful business stands on the foundation of morality."
—HENRY WARD BEECHER

"Hell, there are no rules here—we're trying to accomplish something."
—THOMAS EDISON

A mericans admire ambition and energy in business. Business people aren't slow about letting others known How They Did It. In fact, with all the business advice available, it's surprising that all businesses aren't wildly successful. If someone complains to you about their struggling enterprise, quote them these words of wisdom.

"Good business leaders create a vision, articulate the vision, passionately own the vision, and relentlessly drive it to completion."

—JACK WELCH

"The success combination in business is: Do what you do better . . . and do more of what you do."

—DAVID JOSEPH SCHWARTZ

"Failure is simply the opportunity to begin again, this time more intelligently."

—HENRY FORD (1863–1947)
founder of the Ford Motor Company, epitomized the early twentieth-century American industrialist.

"In the end, all business operations can be reduced to three words: people, product, and profits. Unless you've got a good team, you can't do much with the other two."

—LEE IACOCCA

"To succeed in business it is necessary to make others see things as you see them."

—JOHN H. PATTERSON

"Executive ability is deciding quickly and getting somebody else to do the work."

—EARL NIGHTINGALE

"The most successful businessman is the man who holds onto the old just as long as it is good and grabs the new just as soon as it is better."

—LEE IACOCCA

"A cardinal principle of Total Quality escapes too many managers: you cannot continuously improve interdependent systems and processes until you progressively perfect interdependent, interpersonal relationships."

—STEPHEN COVEY

"The final test of a leader is that he leaves behind him in other men the conviction and the will to carry on."

—WALTER LIPPMANN

"It is not the employer who pays the wages. He only handles the money. It is the product that pays the wages."

—HENRY FORD

"Effective leadership is putting first things first. Effective management is discipline, carrying it out."

—STEPHEN COVEY

"Obstacles are those frightful things you see when you take your eyes off your goal."

—HENRY FORD

"The buck stops with the guy who signs the checks."

—RUPERT MURDOCH

"Almost all quality improvement comes via simplification of design, manufacturing . . . layout, processes, and procedures."

—TOM PETERS (1942–)
is a well-known business writer and speaker. His book *In Search of Excellence* is today considered a business classic.

There are some who are a good deal more cynical about business and executives than others. If an MBA of your acquaintance gets a swelled head, bring her or him down to earth with one of these.

"In college, Yuppies major in business administration. If to meet certain requirements they have to take a liberal arts course, they take Business Poetry."

—DAVE BARRY

"Competition brings out the best in products and the worst in people."

—DAVID SARNOFF (1891–1971) was a pioneer of early television and founder of the National Broadcasting Company.

"About the time we can make the ends meet, somebody moves the ends."

—HERBERT HOOVER

"Informed decision-making comes from a long tradition of guessing and then blaming others for inadequate results."

—SCOTT ADAMS

"An advertising agency is 85 percent confusion and 15 percent commission."

—FRED ALLEN

"Corporation, n. An ingenious device for obtaining individual profit without individual responsibility."

—AMBROSE BIERCE

"I find it rather easy to portray a businessman. Being bland, rather cruel, and incompetent comes naturally to me."

—JOHN CLEESE

"Remind people that profit is the difference between revenue and expense. This makes you look smart."

—SCOTT ADAMS (1957–) from the vantage point of his daily comic strip *Dilbert* chronicles the insanities of cubicle life.

"Give a man a fish and he will eat for a day. Teach a man to fish and he will eat for a lifetime. Teach a man to create an artificial shortage of fish and he will eat steak."

—JAY LENO

In the end we rely on innovation and know-how to get us through any business crisis, led by executives who are strong, smart, capable, and—we hope—ethical. To keep yourself grounded, and to remind others of the importance of honesty in business, quote from this selection of thoughts.

"To open a shop is easy; to keep it open is an art."

—CHINESE PROVERB

"It is difficult but not impossible to conduct strictly honest business."

—MOHANDAS GANDHI

"In the business world, the rearview mirror is always clearer than the windshield."

—WARREN BUFFETT (1930–) is America's foremost investor and one of the richest men in the world.

"I buy when other people are selling."

—JOHN PAUL GETTY

"Government 'help' to business is just as disastrous as government persecution . . . . The only way a government can be of service to national prosperity is by keeping its hands off."

—AYN RAND

"Economic depression cannot be cured by legislative action or executive pronouncement. Economic wounds must be healed by the action of the cells of the economic body—the producers and consumers themselves."

—HERBERT HOOVER

"And while the law of competition may be sometimes hard for the individual, it is best for the race, because it ensures the survival of the fittest in every department."

—ANDREW CARNEGIE

"It is not from the benevolence of the butcher, the brewer, or the baker that we expect our dinner, but from their regard to their own interest."

—ADAM SMITH (1723–1790) was a Scottish economist whose book *The Wealth of Nations* set out the basic elements of the capitalist system.

"If you owe the bank $100 that's your problem. If you owe the bank $100 million, that's the bank's problem."

—JOHN PAUL GETTY

"A business that makes nothing but money is a poor business."

—HENRY FORD

"Drive thy business, let not that drive thee."

—BENJAMIN FRANKLIN

"Sometimes when you innovate, you make mistakes. It is best to admit them quickly, and get on with improving your other innovations."

—STEVE JOBS

"The first rule of any technology used in a business is that automation applied to an efficient operation will magnify the efficiency. The second is that automation applied to an inefficient operation will magnify the inefficiency."

—BILL GATES

"If you cannot work with love but only with distaste, it is better that you should leave your work."

—KAHLIL GIBRAN

"I want to put a ding in the universe."

—STEVE JOBS (1955–)
founder and CEO of Apple Computers, is considered to be on the cutting edge of innovation in information technology.

"I understand small business growth. I was one."

—GEORGE W. BUSH

TECHNOLOGY

Ever since cavemen began to bang rocks together, humans have been fascinated and repelled by technology. Even then, there were probably other cavemen who complained that rock banging would lead to Bad Things and that the noise kept them up at night after a hard day of hunting sabertooth tigers. On the other hand, others were busy developing Banging Rocks 2.0—Now with Special Sabertooth Tiger Stunning App. Since then, the debate has only intensified as we've felt ourselves more and more at the mercy of our inventions. If you find yourself standing with a group of R&D engineers, all of them pontificating about the revolutionary features of their new software system, use one of these quotations to remind them of the triviality of their work.

"All of the biggest technological inventions created by man—the airplane, the automobile, the computer—says little about his intelligence, but speaks volumes about his laziness."

—MARK KENNEDY

"Inventor, n. A person who makes an ingenious arrangement of wheels, levers and springs, and believes it civilization."

—AMBROSE BIERCE

"It has become appallingly obvious that our technology has exceeded our humanity."

—ALBERT EINSTEIN

"If it keeps up, man will atrophy all his limbs but the push-button finger."

—FRANK LLOYD WRIGHT

"Soon silence will have passed into legend. Man has turned his back on silence. Day after day he invents machines and devices that increase noise and distract humanity from the essence of life, contemplation, meditation . . . tooting, howling, screeching, booming, crashing, whistling, grinding, and trilling bolster his ego. His anxiety subsides. His inhuman void spreads monstrously like a gray vegetation."

—JEAN ARP

"Technological progress has merely provided us with more efficient means for going backwards."

—ALDOUS HUXLEY

"The drive toward complex technical achievement offers a clue to why the U.S. is good at space gadgetry and bad at slum problems."

—JOHN KENNETH GALBRAITH

"Once upon a time we were just plain people. But that was before we began having relationships with mechanical systems. Get involved with a machine and sooner or later you are reduced to a factor."

—ELLEN GOODMAN (1941–) is an American journalist and columnist. She retired from writing her syndicated column in 2010.

"It is questionable if all the mechanical inventions yet made have lightened the day's toil of any human being."

—JOHN STUART MILL

"We are becoming the servants in thought, as in action, of the machine we have created to serve us."

—JOHN KENNETH GALBRAITH

Of all our inventions, computers scare us the most. Whether it's Hal in *2001: A Space Odyssey* taking over the space ship and trying to kill the astronauts . . . or the supercomputer in *WarGames* trying to start a war with the Soviet Union . . . or Arnold Schwarzenegger, back from the future to destroy the hope of the human race . . . . Computers seem to be something that could easily get out of control. Lest computer programmers in your vicinity wax too enthusiastic about the newest products of Microsoft and Apple, have one of the following quotations ready to take the wind out of their sails.

"The real danger is not that computers will begin to think like men, but that men will begin to think like computers."

—SYDNEY J. HARRIS

"One day soon the Gillette company will announce the development of a razor that, thanks to a computer microchip, can actually travel ahead in time and shave beard hairs that don't even exist yet."

—DAVE BARRY

"A computer is like an Old Testament god, with a lot of rules and no mercy."

—JOSEPH CAMPBELL

"Where is all the knowledge we lost with information?"

—T. S. ELIOT

"Computers make it easier to do a lot of things, but most of the things they make it easier to do don't need to be done."

—ANDY ROONEY

"Computers are useless. They can only give you answers."

—PABLO PICASSO

"Computer dating is fine if you're a computer."

—RITA MAE BROWN (1944–)
is a novelist whose early novel, *Rubyfruit Jungle,* was one of the first to bring lesbianism into mainstream literature.

"To err is human, but to really foul things up, you need a computer."

—PAUL ERLICH

Naturally, there are people who are much more optimistic about computers and their role in society. Not too surprisingly, a lot of these people work in the information technology industry. But it's worthwhile to have some of their comments handy on your laptop.

"The number one benefit of information technology is that it empowers pcople to do what they want to do. It lets people be creative. It lets people be productive. It lets people learn things they didn't think they could learn before, and so in a sense it is all about potential."

—STEVE BALLMER

"It's a fact that more people watch television and get their information that way than read books. I find new technology and new ways of communication very exciting and would like to do more in this field."

—STEPHEN COVEY

"Information technology and business are becoming inextricably interwoven. I don't think anybody can talk meaningfully about one without the talking about the other."

—BILL GATES

"The Internet is the Viagra of big business."

—JACK WELCH (1935–)
was CEO of General Electric
for almost two decades.

"There might be new technology, but technological progress itself was nothing new—and over the years it had not destroyed jobs, but created them."

—MARGARET THATCHER

"Technology is a gift of God. After the gift of life, it is perhaps the greatest of God's gifts. It is the mother of civilizations, of arts, and of sciences."

—FREEMAN DYSON

"If GM had kept up with technology like the computer industry has, we would all be driving $25 cars that got 1,000 MPG."

—BILL GATES

"The science of today is the technology of tomorrow."

—EDWARD TELLER

"The technologies which have had the most profound effects on human life are usually simple."

—Freeman Dyson

Still, after all is said and done and despite our technological advancements and inclinations, we face the future with a certain nervousness. If you want to sound appropriately anxious about the future of the planet and of humanity, remember these thoughts.

"For a successful technology, reality must take precedence over public relations, for Nature cannot be fooled."

—Richard P. Feynman

"Technology . . . is a queer thing. It brings you great gifts with one hand, and it stabs you in the back with the other."

—C. P. Snow

"The system of nature, of which man is a part, tends to be self-balancing, self-adjusting, self-cleansing. Not so with technology."

—E. F. Schumacher

"I am sorry to say that there is too much point to the wisecrack that life is extinct on other planets because their scientists were more advanced than ours."

—JOHN F. KENNEDY

"Humanity is acquiring all the right technology for all the wrong reasons."

—R. BUCKMINSTER FULLER

"The greatest task before civilization at present is to make machines what they ought to be, the slaves, instead of the masters of men."

—HAVELOCK ELLIS (1859–1939)
British sex theorist and activist, was one of the first to believe that homosexuality was not a disease.

"You cannot endow even the best machine with initiative; the jolliest steam-roller will not plant flowers."

—WALTER LIPPMANN

"We live in a society exquisitely dependent on science and technology, in which hardly anyone knows anything about science and technology."

—CARL SAGAN

"If we continue to develop our technology without wisdom or prudence, our servant may prove to be our executioner."

—OMAR BRADLEY

"The real problem is not whether machines think but whether men do."

—B. F. SKINNER

"There are three roads to ruin: women, gambling, and technicians. The most pleasant is with women, the quickest is with gambling, but the surest is with technicians."

—GEORGES POMPIDOU

"Lo! Men have become the tools of their tools."

—HENRY DAVID THOREAU

"God never made his work for man to mend."

—JOHN DRYDEN

"Technology. No place for wimps."

—SCOTT ADAMS

PART IX

RELIGION

"Religion is what an individual does
with his solitariness."

—ALFRED NORTH WHITEHEAD

RELIGION

Religion is one subject that can be counted upon to start arguments, break up friendships, and occasionally to begin wars. This isn't surprising; it deals with deeply held beliefs that affect the most basic ways in which we live. When the discussion around the dinner table turns to religion and voices begin to rise or chairs are pushed back, have some calming quotations ready to throw into the mix so that tempers can cool.

"True religion is real living; living with all one's soul, with all one's goodness and righteousness."

—ALBERT EINSTEIN

"The highest knowledge is to know that we are surrounded by mystery. Neither knowledge nor hope for the future can be the pivot of our life or determine its direction. It is intended to be solely determined by our allowing ourselves to be gripped by the ethical God, who reveals Himself in us, and by our yielding our will to His."

—ALBERT SCHWEITZER

"I have an everyday religion that works for me. Love yourself first, and everything else falls into line."

—LUCILLE BALL

"The true meaning of religion is thus not simply morality, but morality touched by emotion."

—MATTHEW ARNOLD
(1822–1888)
poet and critic, was widely regarded both for his writings and for his pleasant character.

"Being religious means asking passionately the question of the meaning of our existence and being willing to receive answers, even if the answers hurt."

—PAUL TILLICH

"As to the gods, I have no means of knowing either that they exist or do not exist."

—PROTAGORAS

"Religion without humanity is very poor human stuff."

—SOJOURNER TRUTH

"God made so many different kinds of people. Why would he allow only one way to serve him?"

—MARTIN BUBER

"This is my simple religion. There is no need for temples; no need for complicated philosophy. Our own brain, our own heart is our temple; the philosophy is kindness."

—DALAI LAMA

I ntellectuals, on the whole, have tended to distrust religion, especially during the past century. If you're looking for something snippy to say about religious beliefs— though not necessarily about one particular religion—consider one of the following.

"But who prays for Satan? Who, in eighteen centuries, has had the common humanity to pray for the one sinner that needed it most?"

—MARK TWAIN

"Scriptures, n. The sacred books of our holy religion, as distinguished from the false and profane writings on which all other faiths are based."

—AMBROSE BIERCE

"Religion is a monumental chapter in the history of human egotism."

—WILLIAM JAMES (1842–1910) psychologist and philosopher, was the brother of the novelist Henry James.

"If God has created us in His image, we have more than returned the compliment."

—VOLTAIRE

"Lighthouses are more helpful than churches."

—BENJAMIN FRANKLIN

"Men never do evil so completely and cheerfully as when they do it from religious conviction."

—BLAISE PASCAL

"A deist is someone who has not lived long enough to become an atheist."

—DENIS DIDEROT

"If the concept of God has any validity or any use, it can only be to make us larger, freer, and more loving. If God cannot do this, then it is time we got rid of Him."

—JAMES BALDWIN (1924–1987) was an African American novelist, playwright, political activist, and author of *Go Tell It on the Mountain* and *Another Country*.

"We have just enough religion to make us hate, but not enough to make us love."

—JONATHAN SWIFT

"In religion and politics people's beliefs and convictions are in almost every case gotten at second-hand, and without examination, from authorities who have not themselves examined the questions at issue but have taken them at second-hand from other non-examiners, whose opinions about them were not worth a brass farthing."

—MARK TWAIN

"If God did not exist it would be necessary for us to invent Him."

—VOLTAIRE

"It is wonderful how much time good people spend fighting the devil. If they would only expend the same amount of energy loving their fellow men, the devil would die in his own tracks of ennui."

—HELEN KELLER

"All religions, with their gods, their demi-gods, and their prophets, their messiahs and their saints, were created by the prejudiced fancy of men who had not attained the full development and full possession of their faculties."

—MIKHAIL BAKUNIN

"The religion of one age is the literary entertainment of the next."

—RALPH WALDO EMERSON

K arl Marx's famous comment that religion is the opiate of the people is sometimes interpreted as a slur against Christianity. In point of fact, Marx was actually talking about religion in general. (If you consider that opium makes its users feel better, at least in the short run, Marx's comments could also be interpreted as a positive sentiment about religion.) But plenty of others have criticized the lack of Christian spirit among Christians. If you find yourself in a room full of True Believers, all fulminating about the sinfulness of mainstream Christians, stop them by quoting from the following:

"Christianity might be a good thing if anyone ever tried it."

—GEORGE BERNARD SHAW

"Religious suffering is at one and the same time the expression of real suffering and a protest against real suffering. Religion is the sigh of the oppressed creature, the heart of a heartless world and the soul of soulless conditions. It is the opiate of the people."

—KARL MARX

"Puritanism: the haunting fear that someone, somewhere, may be happy."

—H. L. MENCKEN

"The secret of a good sermon is to have a good beginning and a good ending, then having the two as close together as possible."

—GEORGE BURNS

"A cult is a religion with no political power."

—TOM WOLFE (1931–)
is an American writer and journalist known for such nonfiction books of reportage as *The Right Stuff* and for novels such as *Bonfire of the Vanities*.

D espite opposition over the years, a good number of people have found positive things to say about both religion and the need for a religion that doesn't tell its followers to hate someone else. You can close out a discussion of religion by giving your listeners something to think about.

"I always like a dog so long as he isn't spelled backward."

—G. K. CHESTERTON

"Although he's regularly asked to do so, God does not take sides in American politics."

—GEORGE MITCHELL

"Did St. Francis really preach to the birds? Whatever for? If he really liked birds he would have done better to preach to the cats."

—REBECCA WEST

"Doubt is part of all religion. All the religious thinkers were doubters."

— ISAAC BASHEVIS SINGER

"Religion either makes men wise and virtuous, or it makes them set up false pretences to both."

— WILLIAM HAZLITT

"If I were personally to define religion, I would say that it is a bandage that man has invented to protect a soul made bloody by circumstances."

— THEODORE DREISER

(1871–1945)

was an American novelist whose works created searing psychological portraits of the protagonists.

"Aim at heaven and you will get earth thrown in. Aim at earth and you get neither."

— C. S. LEWIS

"I would rather live my life as if there is a God and die to find out there isn't, than live my life as if there isn't and die to find out there is."

— ALBERT CAMUS

"Religion is essentially the art and the theory of the remaking of man. Man is not a finished creation."

— EDMUND BURKE

"A man's ethical behavior should be based effectually on sympathy, education, and social ties and needs; no religious basis is necessary. Man would indeed be in a poor way if he had to be restrained by fear of punishment and hope of reward after death."

— ALBERT EINSTEIN

"I am determined that my children shall be brought up in their father's religion if they can find out what it is."

— CHARLES LAMB

"It is in our lives and not our words that our religion must be read."

— THOMAS JEFFERSON

"Everyone ought to worship God according to his own inclinations and not to be constrained by force."

—FLAVIUS JOSEPHUS (37–100) was a historian of the early Roman Empire.

"To die for a religion is easier than to live it absolutely."

—JORGE LUIS BORGES

"The point is, could God pass an examination in Theology?"

—MALCOLM MUGGERIDGE

"Religion is what keeps the poor from murdering the rich."

—NAPOLEON BONAPARTE

"When men destroy their old gods they will find new ones to take their place."

—PEARL S. BUCK

Perhaps the poet Kahlil Gibran said it best:

"I love you when you bow in your mosque, kneel in your temple, pray in your church. For you and I are sons of one religion, and it is the spirit."

—KAHLIL GIBRAN

DEATH

"In this world, nothing can be said to be certain but death and taxes." This quote, which is doubtfully attributed to Benjamin Franklin, encapsulates the dilemma of the human condition: no matter how ingenious we are, no matter how much money we make, no matter how good or bad a life we lead, no matter how we ring ourselves round with the miracles of medicine and religion, death comes for us all.

Thus we—as expressed in the following quotes—confront death by defying it, laughing at it, or rationalizing it . . . or sometimes all three at once.

"Death? Why this fuss about death. Use your imagination, try to visualize a world without death! . . . Death is the essential condition of life, not an evil."

—CHARLOTTE PERKINS GILMAN
(1860–1935)
wrote "The Yellow Wallpaper," a classic short story of madness, which later became a key feminist document.

"Down, down, down into the darkness of the grave

Gently they go, the beautiful, the tender, the kind;

Quietly they go, the intelligent, the witty, the brave.

I know. But I do not approve. And I am not resigned."

—EDNA ST. VINCENT MILLAY

"Destroying is a necessary function in life. Everything has its season, and all things eventually lose their effectiveness and die."

—MARGARET J. WHEATLEY

"Do not go gentle into that good night,

Old age should burn and rave at close of day;

Rage, rage against the dying of the light."

—DYLAN THOMAS

"When the gods created man they allotted to him death, but life they retained in their own keeping."

—THE EPIC OF GILGAMESH

"I went to the woods because I wished to live deliberately, to front only the essential facts of life, and see if I could not learn what it had to teach, and not, when I came to die, discover that I have not lived."

—HENRY DAVID THOREAU

"Thus that which is the most awful of evils, death, is nothing to us, since when we exist there is no death, and when there is death we do not exist."

—EPICURUS

"The goal of all life is death."

—SIGMUND FREUD (1856–1939) is regarded as a seminal figure in the development of Modernist culture, although many of his scientific theories have been discredited.

"Oh, for the time when I shall sleep

Without identity."

—EMILY BRONTË

"For death is no more than a turning of us over from time to eternity."

—WILLIAM PENN

"I think we should look forward to death more than we do. Of course everybody hates to go to bed or miss anything but dying is really the only chance we'll get to rest."

—FLORENCE KENNEDY

"Life does not cease to be funny when people die any more than it ceases to be serious when people laugh."

—GEORGE BERNARD SHAW

"There is no cure for birth and death save to enjoy the interval."

—GEORGE SANTAYANA

"Pale Death with impartial tread beats at the poor man's cottage door and at the palaces of kings."

—HORACE (65 BCE–8 BCE) was a Roman lyric poet. His odes are considered one of the literary high points of Rome's Augustan age.

"Death can sneak up on you like a silent kitten, surprising you with its touch and you have a right to act surprised. Other times death stomps in the front door, unwanted and unannounced, and makes its noisy way to your seat on the sofa."

—HUGH ELLIOTT

The worst thing about death, paradoxically, is knowing that we're going to die. A being without awareness beyond the immediate moment of its existence—a frog, say, or a garden slug or Kim Kardashian—is probably pretty content without the knowledge of death to blight its existence. We, on the other hand, have to come to terms with it.

"The fear of death follows from the fear of life. A man who lives fully is prepared to die at any time."

—MARK TWAIN

"The idea of death, the fear of it, haunts the human animal like nothing else; it is a mainspring of human activity—designed largely to avoid the fatality of death, to overcome it by denying in some way that it is the final destiny of man."

—ERNEST BECKER

"Because I could not stop for Death,

He kindly stopped for me.

The Carriage held but just ourselves

And Immortality."

—EMILY DICKINSON

"Life is better than death, I believe, if only because it is less boring and because it has fresh peaches in it."

—ALICE WALKER

"Think not disdainfully of death, but look on it with favor; for even death is one of the things Nature wills."

—MARCUS AURELIUS (121–180)
sometimes called the Philosopher Emperor, wrote *Meditations*, reflecting on human duty and accomplishment.

"Dying is a very dull, dreary affair. And my advice to you is to have nothing whatever to do with it."

—W. SOMERSET MAUGHAM

"Death, the sable smoke where vanishes the flame."

—LORD BYRON

Probably the best approach to death is to enjoy living, because this is about the only chance we're going to get at it. Thus, to someone who's sunk in morbidity, you can always fish out a piece of wisdom the brighten their day and jerk them out of their dark mood.

"Do not fear death so much, but rather the inadequate life."

—BERTOLT BRECHT

"For certain is death for the born

And certain is birth for the dead;

Therefore over the inevitable

Thou shouldst not grieve."

—BHAGAVAD GITA

"I'm not afraid of death. It's the stake one puts up in order to play the game of life."

—JEAN GIRAUDOUX

"Death is a delightful hiding place for weary men."

—HERODOTUS

"There are so many little dyings, it doesn't matter which of them is death."

—KENNETH PATCHEN
(1911–1972)
a poet and novelist, wrote works that reflected Modernist trends on the American scene

"Death may be the greatest of all human blessings."

—SOCRATES

"From my rotting body, flowers shall grow, and I am in them and that is eternity."

—EDVARD MUNCH

"Death is for many of us the gate of hell; but we are inside on the way out, not outside on the way in."

—GEORGE BERNARD SHAW

"Death is a debt we all must pay."

—EURIPIDES

Despite Euripides' comforting words, there's no denying that death can cast a damper on the liveliest of parties. If the conversation around you turns to death and everyone is gloomy and hanging on the edge of their cocktails, silently planning their next visit to an estate planner, cheer things up by saying something such as:

"Religion is the human response to being alive and having to die."

—F. FORRESTER CHURCH

"If my doctor told me I had only six minutes to live, I wouldn't brood. I'd type a little faster."

—ISAAC ASIMOV

"There are worse things in life than death. Have you ever spent an evening with an insurance salesman?"

—WOODY ALLEN

"A man's dying is more the survivors' affair than his own."

—THOMAS MANN

"Let children walk with Nature, let them see the beautiful blendings and communions of death and life, their joyous inseparable unity, as taught in woods and meadows, plains and mountains and streams of our blessed star, and they will learn that death is stingless indeed and as beautiful as life."

—JOHN MUIR (1838–1914) naturalist and cocreator of the Sierra Club, is the founding figure of the American environmental movement.

"I am ready to meet my Maker. Whether my Maker is prepared for the ordeal of meeting me is another matter."

—WINSTON CHURCHILL

"Of all the wonders that I yet have heard,

It seems to me most strange that men should fear;

Seeing that death, a necessary end,

Will come when it will come."

—WILLIAM SHAKESPEARE

"Biography lends to death a new terror."

—OSCAR WILDE

"For what is it to die but to stand in the sun and melt into the wind? And when the Earth has claimed our limbs, then we shall truly dance."

—KAHLIL GIBRAN

"I shall not die of a cold. I shall die of having lived."

—WILLA CATHER (1873–1947)
an American author whose novels depict the harsh life on the frontier., was awarded the Pulitzer Prize for *One of Ours*.

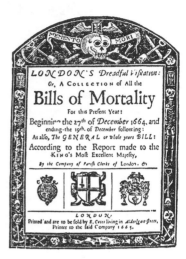

LONDON'S Dreadful Visitation:
Or, A Collection of All the
Bills of Mortality
For this Present Year:
Beginning the 27th of December 1664, and ending the 19th of December following:
As also, The GENERAL or whole years BILL:
According to the Report made to the King's Most Excellent Majesty,
By the Company of Parish Clerks of London, &c

LONDON,
Printed and are to be sold by E. Cotes living in Aldersgate-street, Printer to the said Company 1665.

"Our brains are seventy-year clocks. The Angel of Life winds them up once for all, then closes the case and gives the key into the hand of the Angel of Resurrection."

—OLIVER WENDELL HOLMES

"Tomorrow and tomorrow and tomorrow,

Creeps in this petty pace from day to day

Unto the last syllable of recorded time.

And all our yesterdays have lighted fools the way to dusty death."

—WILLIAM SHAKESPEARE

"Fear not death, for the sooner we die the longer we shall be immortal."

—BENJAMIN FRANKLIN

IMMORTALITY

And what comes after death? Is there something more? Intellectuals (and a lot of other people) have been batting this question around for the past two or three thousand years without arriving at any definitive answer. That hasn't, of course, stopped anyone from having strong opinions on the subject. Remind your listeners that death comes for each of us by dropping one of the following pearls of wisdom.

"Immortality is not a gift.

Immortality is an achievement.

And only those who strive mightily

Shall achieve it."

—EDGAR LEE MASTERS

"Surely God would not have created such a being as man, with an ability to grasp the infinite, to exist only for a day! No, no, man was made for immortality."

—ABRAHAM LINCOLN

"That man has reached immortality who is disturbed by nothing material."

—SWAMI VIVEKANANDA

"The day which we fear as our last is but the birthday of eternity."

—SENECA

"All men's souls are immortal, but the souls of the righteous are immortal and divine."

—SOCRATES

"I intend to live forever. So far, so good."

—STEVEN WRIGHT

I mmortality, many agree, is achieved by what you leave behind: books, good works, children, and so forth. Some people may find it comforting to confront the hereafter if you quote them something like this.

"I don't want to achieve immortality through my work. I want to achieve it through not dying."

—WOODY ALLEN

"For Love is immortality."

—EMILY DICKINSON

(1830–1886)

remained in Amherst, Massachusetts, for most of her life, writing poetry and shunning human contact.

"Children are the only form of immortality that we can be sure of."

—PETER USTINOV

"Poets have said that the reason to have children is to give yourself immortality. Immortality? Now that I have five children, my only hope is that they are all out of the house before I die."

—BILL COSBY

"I don't believe in personal immortality; the only way I expect to have some version of such a thing is through my books."

—ISAAC ASIMOV

"I've put in so many enigmas and puzzles [in my books] that it will keep the professors busy for centuries arguing over what I meant, and that's the only way of insuring one's immortality."

—JAMES JOYCE

"If I have any beliefs about immortality, it is that certain dogs I have known will go to heaven, and very, very few persons."

—JAMES THURBER

"If all else fails, immortality can always be assured by spectacular error."

—JOHN KENNETH GALBRAITH

"If your contribution has been vital there will always be somebody to pick up where you left off, and that will be your claim to immortality."

—WALTER GROPIUS

"What a man does for others, not what they do for him, gives him immortality."

—DANIEL WEBSTER

(1782–1852)

was a politician and leader of the Whig Party before its destruction in the years leading up to the Civil War.

"He ne'er is crowned with immortality

Who fears to follow where airy voices lead."

—JOHN KEATS

"When a noble life has prepared old age, it is not decline that it reveals but the first days of immortality."

—MURIEL SPARK

"I shall tell you a great secret, my friend. Do not wait for the last judgment. It takes place every day."

—ALBERT CAMUS

"The key to immortality is first living a life worth remembering."

—BRANDON LEE

S ome authorities are not even sure that immortality is really all that it's cracked up to be. You can show proper cynicism about the prospect of living eternally by quoting along these lines:

"The average man, who does not know what to do with his life, wants another one which will last forever."

—ANATOLE FRANCE (1844–1924)

French novelist and poet, was a champion of political and artistic liberty.

"Do not try to live for ever. You will not succeed."

—GEORGE BERNARD SHAW

"Millions long for immortality who don't know what to do with themselves on a rainy Sunday afternoon."

—SUSAN ERTZ

"Immortality—a fate worse than death."

—EDGAR A. SHOAFF

"A healthy nature needs no God or immortality."

—FRIEDRICH VON SCHILLER

"To desire immortality is to desire the eternal perpetuation of a great mistake."

—ARTHUR SCHOPENHAUER

If we're sure of anything, it's that the best way to ensure immortality is not to recognize our own death. After all, what do dead people know? If you want to scoff in the face of death and show that you're not intimidated by the Grim Reaper, after your fourth or fifth cocktail hurl one of these quotes into the conversation, laughing carelessly as you say it.

"To be immortal is commonplace; except for man, all creatures are immortal, for they are ignorant of death."
—JORGE LUIS BORGES

"A man has only one way of being immortal on earth; he has to forget he is a mortal."
—JEAN GIRAUDOUX (1882–1944)
French novelist and playwright, wrote primarily active between World War I and World War II.

"Immortality is the condition of a dead man who doesn't believe he is dead."
—H. L. MENCKEN

Some great thinkers have suggested that the afterlife is just a continuation of our present life. Thus we can go on forever, just as we are now. And to some, that may be a comforting thought. Encourage your listeners that there may be hope for immortality by citing something like these thoughts.

"One of the strange things about living in the world is that it is only now and then one is quite sure one is going to live forever and ever and ever. One knows it sometimes when one gets up at the tender solemn dawn-time and goes out and stands alone and throws one's head far back and looks up and up and watches the pale sky slowly changing and flushing and marvelous unknown things happening until the East almost makes one cry out and one's heart stands still at the strange unchanging majesty of the rising of the sun—which has been happening every morning for thousands and thousands and thousands of years. One knows it then for a moment or so . . . ."

—FRANCES BURNETT

"A graceful and honorable old age is the childhood of immortality."

—PINDAR

"Life is the childhood of our immortality."

—JOHANN WOLFGANG VON GOETHE

"The union of the Word and the Mind produces that mystery which is called Life . . . . Learn deeply of the Mind and its mystery, for therein lies the secret of immortality."

—JOSEPH ADDISON

"People always live forever when there is an annuity to be paid them."

—JANE AUSTEN

"I am like a falling star who has finally found her place next to another in a lovely constellation, where we will sparkle in the heavens forever."

—AMY TAN

Happiness

"Happiness," said Aristotle, "is the meaning and the purpose of life, the whole aim and the end of human existence."

By and large, most people would agree with this statement. The problem comes in trying to figure out what we each mean by "happiness." Is it big or small, selfish or altruistic, fleeting or permanent? There are as many opinions on the subject as there've been people to have them. You can show your listeners that you've meditated long and vigorously on the subject by murmuring a few words from one of the great thinkers here cited.

"Happiness is not being pained in body or troubled in mind."
—Thomas Jefferson

"Happiness belongs to the self-sufficient."
—Aristotle

"That man is richest whose pleasures are cheapest."
—Henry David Thoreau

"The truest greatness lies in being kind, the truest wisdom in a happy mind."
—Ella Wheeler Wilcox
(1850–1919)
American poet.

"There is only one happiness in life, to love and be loved."
—George Sand

"Happiness is having a large, loving, caring, close-knit family in another city."
—George Burns

"Happiness? That's nothing more than health and a poor memory."
—Albert Schweitzer

"Happiness is not a goal; it is a by-product."
—Eleanor Roosevelt

"Happiness is a butterfly which, when pursued, is always just beyond your grasp but which, if you will sit down quietly, may alight upon you."
—Nathaniel Hawthorne

"Happiness is your dentist telling you it won't hurt and then having him catch his hand in the drill."

—JOHNNY CARSON

S o how can you get happiness? Intellectuals agree it doesn't come from money or material possessions—which should be comforting to those who lack either—but they're divided on what creates happiness. They're not even united on whether one should strive to be happy. Since conversations often wind their way to this dilemma, have a quotation handy on the subject to round out the discussion and bring it to a more or less successful conclusion.

"If you want to live a happy life, tie it to a goal, not to people or things."

—ALBERT EINSTEIN

"There is only one way to happiness, and that is to cease worrying about things which are beyond the power of our will."

—EPICTETUS

"The greatest happiness you can have is knowing that you do not necessarily require happiness."

—WILLIAM SAROYAN
(1908–1981)
novelist and playwright, wrote stories about the immigrant experience, including the charming *My Name is Aram*.

"Eden is that old-fashioned house we dwell in every day

Without suspecting our abode until we drive away."

—EMILY DICKINSON

"It is not easy to find happiness in ourselves, and it is not possible to find it elsewhere."

—AGNES REPPLIER

"The secret of happiness is freedom. The secret of freedom is courage."

—THUCYDIDES

"If one advances confidently in the direction of one's dreams, and endeavors to live the life which one has imagined, one will meet with a success unexpected in common hours."

—HENRY DAVID THOREAU

"Sanity and happiness are an impossible combination."

—MARK TWAIN

"Life is made up of small pleasures. Happiness is made up of those tiny successes. The big ones come too infrequently. And if you don't collect all these tiny successes, the big ones don't really mean anything."

—NORMAN LEAR (1922–)
television producer, was responsible for such beloved classics as *All in the Family*, *The Jeffersons*, *Good Times*, and *Sanford and Son*.

"The Constitution only guarantees the American people the right to pursue happiness. You have to catch it yourself."

—BENJAMIN FRANKLIN

"The pursuit of happiness is a most ridiculous phrase: if you pursue happiness you'll never find it."

—C. P. SNOW

"The best way to cheer yourself up is to try to cheer somebody else up."

—MARK TWAIN

"If only we'd stop trying to be happy we could have a pretty good time."

—EDITH WHARTON

"To be happy, we must not be too concerned with others."

—ALBERT CAMUS (1913–1960) received the Nobel Prize for literature in 1957. His novels include *The Stranger* and *The Plague*.

"Happiness is when what you think, what you say, and what you do are in harmony."

—MOHANDAS GANDHI

"Happiness: We rarely feel it.

I would buy it, beg it, steal it,

Pay in coins of dripping blood

For this one transcendent good."

—AMY LOWELL

"If you want to be happy, be."

—LEO TOLSTOY

"Now and then it's good to pause in our pursuit of happiness and just be happy."

—GUILLAUME APOLLINAIRE

"Nothing can bring you to happiness but yourself."

—RALPH WALDO EMERSON

"My advice to you is not to inquire why or whither, but just enjoy your ice cream while it's on your plate."

—THORNTON WILDER

O ther people can contribute to our happiness—either by their presence or absence. Show your appreciation by quoting the likes of Proust, Frost, and Buddha.

"Let us be grateful to people who make us happy, they are the charming gardeners who make our souls blossom."
—MARCEL PROUST (1871–1922) was the author of *Remembrance of Things Past*, a rambling novel in seven books, more referred to than read.

"Happiness makes up in height for what it lacks in length."
—ROBERT FROST

"Thousands of candles can be lighted from a single candle, and the life of the candle will not be shortened. Happiness never decreases by being shared."
—BUDDHA

"Some cause happiness wherever they go; others whenever they go."
—OSCAR WILDE

The art of being happy, you may conclude, lies in understanding what makes you happy and then doing it. That seems simpler in theory than it is in practice, but you may be able to derive some satisfaction in contemplating these thoughts about happiness.

"The moments of happiness we enjoy take us by surprise. It is not that we seize them but that they seize us."

—ASHLEY MONTAGU

"A happy person is not a person in a certain set of circumstances but rather a person with a certain set of attitudes."

—HUGH DOWNS

"When one door of happiness closes, another opens; but often we look so long at the closed door that we do not see the one which has been opened for us."

—HELEN KELLER

"Man is fond of counting his troubles, but he does not count his joys. If he counted them up as he ought to, he would see that every lot has enough happiness provided for it."

—FYODOR DOSTOEVSKY

(1821–1881)

a Russian novelist, is considered second to only Leo Tolstoy as Russia's greatest writer.

"Can anything be so elegant as to have few wants, and to serve them one's self?"

—RALPH WALDO EMERSON

"Pleasure is spread through the earth

In stray gifts to be claimed by whoever shall find."

—WILLIAM WORDSWORTH

"Just as a cautious businessman avoids investing all his capital in one concern, so wisdom would probably admonish us also not to anticipate all our happiness from one quarter alone."

—SIGMUND FREUD

"There are some days when I think I'm going to die from an overdose of satisfaction."

—SALVADOR DALI

"We are no longer happy so soon as we wish to be happier."

—WALTER SAVAGE LANDOR

"One should be either sad or joyful. Contentment is a warm sty for eaters and sleepers."

—EUGENE O'NEILL

"Happiness always looks small while you hold it in your hands, but let it go, and you learn at once how big and precious it is."

—MAXIM GORKY (1868–1936) was a Russian author whose personal and literary reputation was compromised by his association with Stalin's regime

"The essence of philosophy is that a man should so live that his happiness shall depend as little as possible on external things."

—EPICTETUS

"Happiness is a matter of one's most ordinary and everyday mode of consciousness being busy and lively and unconcerned with self."

—IRIS MURDOCH

"What a wonderful life I've had! I only wish I'd realized it sooner."

—COLETTE

AFTERWORD

66 A witty saying," Voltaire remarked sourly,
"proves nothing." And he may be right. Wit is
an inadequate substitute for wisdom—although
these days both seem to be in short supply. However, dear reader, as you have browsed through
this collection I hope you have realized that there
is beauty in a well-turned phrase and wisdom in a
happy epigram.

It may be that you yourself will, in time, become one of the notable
quotables included herewith (it used to be a sign of intellectual emi-
nence to be listed in *Bartlett's Quotations*. Alas, now the Internet has
made that less of a distinction, since there are so many places where
one's bon mots can appear).

As to using quotations to sound like an intellectual, remember that
quoting is an art. Benjamin Disraeli—politician, novelist, and social
butterfly—remarked aptly, "The art of quotation requires more delicacy
in the practice than those conceive who can see nothing more in a quotation than an extract." To quote like an intellectual requires more than
blundering into a conversation, bristling with funny sayings from Oscar
Wilde or pungent comments made by Plutarch. There is an exquisite

daintiness in precisely choosing the right moment to casually remark, "As Alan Bennett says, 'Life is like a tin of sardines; we're all of us looking for the key.'"

Here's hoping that within this distilled collection of the wisdom of the ages you've found the key—to sounding smart.

INDEX

Acton, Lord, 138
Actors, 21
Adams, Abigail, 141
Adams, Henry, 105, 131
Adams, Scott, 193, 201
Addison, Joseph, 222
Aeschylus (Greek tragic dramatist), 17, 101, 145
Aesop (Greek fabulist), 91
Albee, Edward, 44, 49
Alcott, A. Bronson, 169
Alighieri, Dante, 170
Allen, Fred, 36, 193
Allen, Woody, 25, 27, 153, 156, 157, 216, 219
Allende, Isabel, 158
Amory, Cleveland, 68
Angelis, Barbara de, 123
Angelou, Maya, 108, 181
Animals, 184–88
Anouilh, Jean, 142
Apollinaire, Guillaume, 8, 226
Appleton, Edward, 66
Arafat, Yassir, 127
Arbus, Diane, 115
Archimedes (Greek physicist), 76
Architecture, 5–9
Arendt, Hannah, 90
Aristophanes (Greek philologist), 2
Aristotle (Greek philosopher)
    on business, 190
    on education, 165
    on friendship, 125, 129
    on happiness, 223
    on history, 103
    on knowledge, 132, 137
    on mathematics, 84
    on nature, 183
    on politics, 87
    on war, 99

Armstrong, Louis, 4
Arnold, Matthew, 204
Arp, Jean, 17, 196
Art, 1–30
    architecture as, 5–9
    cinema as, 20–30
    painting as, 10–13
    sculpture as, 14–19
Asimov, Isaac, 73, 77, 79, 132, 216, 219
Asquith, Violet, xi
Attenborough, Richard, 22
Auden, W. H., 41, 66, 129
Augustine, Saint, 99
Aurelius, Marcus, 171, 214
Austen, Jane, 33, 115, 162, 177, 222

Bacall, Lauren, 146
Bacon, Francis, 81, 118, 133, 151, 171, 174, 182
Bacon, Roger, 84
Bakunin, Mikhail, 62, 207
Baldwin, James, 106, 206
Baldwin, Stanley, 98
Ball, Lucille, 204
Ballard, J. G., 35
Ballmer, Steve, 199
Balzac, Honoré de, 119
Bankhead, Tallulah, 47
Bardot, Brigitte, 147
Barrows, Allison, 38
Barry, Dave, 53, 67, 76, 95, 149, 193, 198
Barrymore, Ethel, 127
Barrymore, John, 114, 147, 156
Baudelaire, Charles, 43, 162
Beauvoir, Simone de, 158
Bebel, August, 101
Becker, Ernest, 214
Beecher, Henry Ward, 129, 179, 190

Einstein, Albert
  on education, 165
  on fame, 173
  on happiness, 225
  on knowledge, 132, 137
  on love, 114
  on mathematics, 81, 83, 84, 85
  on money, 152
  on nature, 177
  on physics, 75
  on power, 140
  on religion, 204, 210
  on technology, 196
  on war, 99, 100
Eisenhower, Dwight D., 98
Eliot, George, 57, 61, 93, 124, 125,
  130, 184
Eliot, T. S., 42, 146, 198
Elliott, Hugh, 213
Ellis, Havelock, 201
Ellis, Henry, 162
Ellison, Harlan, 156
Emerson, Ralph Waldo
  on fame, 173
  on friendship, 125, 126
  on happiness, 227, 228
  on knowledge, 133
  on language, 50
  on money, 151
  on nature, 175, 177, 179
  on old age, 150
  on power, 139
  on religion, 207
  on science, 72
  on sculpture, 17
Eminem, 172
English proverb, 62
Ephron, Nora, 186
Epictetus (philosopher), 134, 165,
  225, 229
Epicurus (Greek philosopher), 213
Erasmus, Desiderius, 171
Erlich, Paul, 198
Erskine, Ralph, 7
Ertz, Susan, 220
Euclid (Greek mathematician), 83
Euripides (Greek dramatist), 117, 215,
  216

Feiffer, Jules, 158
Fellini, Federico, 2, 28
Fermi, Enrico, 133
Feynman, Richard P., 79, 200
Fiedler, Leslie, 32
Fields, W. C., 153, 163, 184
Fitzgerald, F. Scott, 127
Flaubert, Gustave, 51
Flynn, Errol, 155
Fo, Dario, 48
Forbes, Malcolm, 134, 165
Ford, Henry, 103, 191, 192, 195
Forester, C. S., 34
Forster, E. M., 4
Frame, 170–74
France, Anatole, 165, 187, 220
Francis of Assisi, Saint, 185
Frank, Anne, 176
Franklin, Benjamin
  on business, 190, 195
  on death, 212, 217
  on happiness, 226
  on money, 153
  on power, 139
  on religion, 206
  on war, 98
Freud, Sigmund, 186, 228
Friedrich, Georg Wilhelm, 103
Friendship, 125–31
Frost, Robert, 38, 169, 227
Fry, Roger, 63
Fuller, Margaret, 133
Fuller, R. Buckminster, 201
Fuller, Thomas, 8

Gabor, Dennis, 41
Gabor, Zsa Zsa, 159
Gaiman, Neil, 34, 113
Galbraith, John Kenneth, 89, 92, 197,
  219
Galilei, Galileo, 183
Gandhi, Mohandas, 99, 116, 184, 194,
  226
Garrett, Lesley, 66
Gates, Bill, 195, 199
Gaugin, Paul, 10
Gauss, Karl Friedrich, 74, 83
Gehry, Frank, 9
Geisel, Theodore (Dr. Seuss), 115

THE QUOTABLE INTELLECTUAL

Wagner, Richard, 69
Wald, George, 77
Walker, Alice, 142, 178, 187, 214
Walpole, Hugh, 74
War, 97–102
Warhol, Andy, 11, 25
Warren, Robert Penn, 103
Washington, George, 99, 127, 139
Watson, James D., 80
Webster, Daniel, 220
Webster, Noah, 50
Weinberg, Steven, 76, 183
Welch, Jack, 191, 199
Welles, Orson, 20, 49
Wells, H. G., 108, 181
Welty, Eudora, 36
Wesley, John, 136
West, Mae, 161, 163
West, Rebecca, 209
Wharton, Edith, 4, 148, 153, 226
Wheatley, Margaret J., 212
White, Theodore, 144
Whitehead, Alfred North, 2, 12, 82, 203
Whitman, Walt, 164, 180
Whittier, John Greenleaf, 106
Wilcox, Ella Wheeler, 223
Wilczek, Frank, 76, 77
Wilde, Oscar
 on death, 216
 on friendship, 129
 on happiness, 227
 on history, 108
 on knowledge, 132, 134
 on love, 117
 on marriage, 120
 on money, 153
 on music, 61, 62
 on old age, 145, 146
 on philosophy, 111
 on poetry, 41, 43
 on politics, 91
Wilder, Billy, 27
Wilder, Thornton, 183, 187, 226
Williams, Tennessee, 153
Wilson, Colin, 63
Wilson, Woodrow, 130, 143
Wittgenstein, Ludwig, 82
Wodehouse, P. G., 32, 188

Wolfe, Tom, 209
Woolf, Virginia, 32, 33, 51, 130
Woollcott, Alexander, 157
Wordsworth, William, 179, 228
Work, 189–201
 business, 190–95
 technology, 196–201
Wotruba, Fritz, 17
Wren, Christopher, 7
Wright, Frank Lloyd, 5, 68, 177, 196
Wright, Steven, 12, 218
Wynette, Tammy, 172

Yeats, William Butler, 43, 126, 149–50
Yevtushenko, Yevgeny, 41
Yiddish proverb, 184
Youngman, Henny, 118

Zappa, Frank, 11
Zeffirelli, Franco, 65
Zeno (Greek philosopher), 177
Zsigmond, Vilmos, 23

ABOUT THE AUTHOR

P eter Archer is an editor with Adams Media. At various points in his life he has been a college teacher, a factory worker, a political activist, a convenience store clerk, and once had a job cleaning the cages of 100,000 laboratory mice. He is the author of six novels and a dozen short stories. Having graduated from the University of St. Andrews with an M.Litt. in Medieval History, he subscribes to the *New Yorker*, the *New York Review of Books*, and the *Economist*. He keeps a copy of *Dante's Divine Comedy* on his nightstand and reads the *New York Times* every morning. Which makes him as much of a pseudointellectual as he needed to be to write this book.